Political Dialogue of the Friedrich-Ebert-Stiftung

Policy Studies Series No. 1

The New EU-ACP Partnership: Consequences for Eastern and Southern Africa

Francis A.S.T. Matambalya

The New EU-ACP Partnership: Consequences for Eastern and Southern Africa

MKUKI NA NYOTA PUBLISHERS
P.O. BOX 4246, DAR ES SALAAM, TANZANIA

Published for The Friedrich-Ebert-Stiftung by Mkuki na Nyota Publishers, P.O.Box 4246 Dar es Salaam Tanzania.

Copyright © 2001 Friedrich-Ebert-Stiftung, Dar es Salaam, Tanzania.

ISBN 9976-973-845   Mkuki Na Nyota Publishers
ISBN 9987-220-487   Friedrich-Ebert-Stiftung

All rights reserved

Political Dialogue of the Friedrich-Ebert-Stiftung

Series Editor: Dr. Francis A.S.T. Matambalya

The series *Political Dialogue Studies* takes up topical issues which are directly or indirectly relevant to political dynamics in Tanzania. In this context, the dialogues held in regular workshops and the ensuing studies intend to provide a broad-based forum for the discussion of developments in the political spheres (and their *de rigueur* interplays with other spheres), both domestically and internationally, which are relevant for Tanzania. Though focusing on political issues, they transcend the political sphere and embrace issues which, though not of political nature, directly or indirectly impact on political developments in Tanzania. Also, they are intended to incite critical discussions among various stakeholders in Tanzania, as well as between Tanzania and its international partners from both the developing and developed worlds. Finally, by ameliorating consultation, co-operation and co-ordination, they aim at contributing to a better comprehension of the issues at stake, so that informed and coherent policies can be formulated to guide Tanzania's efforts in the political and related spheres.

The series is published at irregular intervals. For further information about this publication please contact the Friedrich-Ebert-Stiftung office in Tanzania.

Table of contents

Glossary of abbreviations and acronyms... 11
Foreword... 14
Preface.. 15

I	**BACKGROUND ISSUES**... 17
1.	**Introduction**.. 18
1.1.	EU-ACP development co-operation on the road to change 18
1.2.	Preliminary reflections on post-Lomé EU-ACP development co-operation 19
1.3.	Aim and structure of the study 19
2.	**EU's proposal to regionalise its co-operation with its ACP associates**... 20
2.1.	Technical implications of regionalising EU-ACP co-operation.................. 20
2.1.1.	Shift of the loci of EU-ACP development co-operation............................ 20
2.1.2.	Asymmetrical liberalisation and differential treatment 21
2.2.	Conceptual base of regionalised co-operation: trade-driven co-operation .. 21
2.3.	Postulated arguments for REPAs.. 22
2.3.1.	Static welfare gains.. 23
2.3.2.	Dynamic gains 23
2.4.	Postulated arguments against REPAs 24
2.4.1.	Potential costs of REPAs 24
	A. Fiscal effects of liberalisation.. 25
	B. Adjustment costs of liberalisation.. 26
	C. Erosion of static welfare gains... 27
	D. Negative dynamic effects of liberalisation on domestic production 27
2.4.2.	Contentious issues regarding REPAs 28
	A. Status of the ACP group... 28
	B. "Geography of regionalisation" 28
	C. Compliance with multilateralism 28
	D. Ambiguity surrounding differentiation 29
	E. Uncertainties regarding the treatment of services................................. 29
	F. Questionable market-related gains 30
	G. Institutional requirements for the enforcement of REPAs.................... 30
	H. Relevance of the REPA studies 30
II	**THE FRAMEWORK AGREEMENT: FROM REPAS TO EPAS** 32
3.	**The framework agreement for EU-ACP co-operation: a brief overview** 33
3.1	Economic partnership as the basis of development co-operation 34
3.1.1.	Theoretical base and practical orientation of the EPA model of development co-operation.. 34
	A. Theoretical base of the EPA model of development co-operation......... 34
	B. Practical orientation of the EPA model of development co-operation .. 35

3.1.2.	Essential pillars of the EPA model of development co-operation	36
	A. Integrated approach to development strategies	36
	B. Political dimension	37
	C. Financial resources	37
4.	**EU-ACP trade within the framework of the EPA model of development co-operation**	**38**
4.1.	Preparatory phase	38
4.2.	Interim phase	39
4.3.	Summarising remarks	39
5.	**The EPA model of development co-operation and the WTO**	**39**
5.1.	WTO compatibility of trade regimes: overview of the general requirements	39
5.1.1.	Core WTO articles relevant for regional trade regimes	40
5.1.2.	Supplementary WTO articles relevant for regional trade regimes	40
5.2.	Necessity to make the regime to guide future EU-ACP trade WTO compatible	41
5.3.	Options to make EPAs WTO compatible: initial reflections	41
5.3.1.	Opting for a WTO consistent convention	42
	A. WTO consistent within the framework of Article XXIV	42
	B. Consistency within the framework of the Enabling Clause	42
5.3.2.	Opting for a WTO inconsistent convention and bargaining for a waiver	42
5.3.3.	Other viable and less contentious considerations	43
5.3.4.	Summarising remarks	44
5.4.	Adequacy of WTO provisions to provide the legal base for a future EU-ACP trade regime and possible areas for reform	44
5.4.1.	Caveats related to Article XXIV	44
5.4.2.	Caveats related to the Enabling Clause	45
5.4.3.	Caveats related to the Waiver	45
6.	**Potential precipitators and hindrances to the implementation of EPAs**	**45**
6.1.	Technical impediments	45
6.2.	Framework for institutional linkages and modalities for preferential treatment	46
7.	**Summary of merits and demerits of the EPA model of development co-operation**	**46**
III	**KEY ISSUES TO BE ADDRESSED BY THE EASTERN AND SOUTHERN AFRICAN STATES IN THE WAKE OF POST-LOMÉ IV EU-ACP CO-OPERATION**	**49**
8.	**Necessary conditions for functional EPAs between the EU and the ACP states**	**50**
8.1.	Clarity of development co-operation agenda	50
8.2.	Adherence to international obligations of the ACP and EU states	50

| 8.3. | Institutional requirements | 51 |

9. Challenges and nebulous issues 51
9.1 Proliferation of integration schemes 52
9.2. Status of COMESA 52
9.3. Prospect of de-linking South Africa from the region 53
9.4. Risk of chronically dysfunctional institutions including the states 53
9.4.1. General remarks on the dysfunctionality of institutions 53
9.4.2. Significance for Eastern and Southern Africa 54
9.4.3. Deficiency in institutions of national unity 55
9.5. Underdeveloped status of integration in the region 56

IV RECOMMENDATIONS AND CONCLUDING REMARKS 57

10. Reconciling the EPA model of development co-operation and the development requirements of Eastern and Southern Africa 58
10.1. Basic considerations 58
10.1.1. "Geography of regionalisation" 59
10.1.2. Modality of ties: multi-tierism 59
    A. Multi-tierism and the EPA concept 59
    B. Multi-tierism and ACP's institutional requirements 60
10.1.3. Functionality of ties: consolidation of regional integration 60
10.2. Strategic considerations to enhance competitiveness 61
10.2.1. Trade competitiveness 61
    A. Sectoral and product coverage of trade 61
    B. Application of asymmetry 62
10.2.2. Overall economic competitiveness 62
    A. Closing the gap in human resources base 62
    B. Closing the gap in the provision of physical infrastructure 62
    C. Improving governance and economic management 63
    D. Empowerment of civil society 63
    E. Consolidating the private sector 63
    F. Enhancing capacity to participate in international fora 63
    G. Addressing social equity concerns 64

11. Eastern and Southern Africa and the "geography of regionalisation" . 65
11.1. Alternative options for linking Eastern and Southern Africa and the EU ... 65
11.1.1. "Degree of regional homogeneity" option: EPAs modelled on existing individual integration schemes 65
11.1.2. "Pan-Africanist" option: EPAs modelled on extended regional base 66
    A. "Pan-Africanist" option 1: co-operation under the "extended" SADC umbrella 67
    B. "Pan-Africanist" option 2: co-operation under "extended" context of Eastern and Southern Africa 67
11.2. Summarising remarks 68

12. Concluding remarks 68

V APPENDIXES..71

Appendix I : Proposed multi-tier regionally differentiated EU-ACP linkages........72
Appendix II : Key staff requirements of a reformed ACP secretariat......................73
Appendix III: The Cotonou Agreement and what it means for Tanzania................74
    A. What is it the Cotonou Agreement about? 74
    B. Why was a new agreement needed? 74
    C. What are the pillars of the Cotonou Agreement? 75
    D. What will it mean for Tanzania? 75
    E. Some critical views..76

Selected references...77

About the Author and Series Editor..82

Policy Dialogue Papers of the Friedrich-Ebert-Stiftung, Tanzania.................82

Glossary of abbreviations and acronyms

ACP	African, Caribbean and Pacific states; associated with the EU through the LC.
AEC	African Economic Community.
ASEAN	Association of South East Asian Nations.
BENELUX	Belgium, Netherlands and Luxembourg.
BLNS	Botswana, Lesotho, Namibia, Swaziland (associated with South Africa through the SACU).
CAP	Common Agricultural Policy (of the EU).
CARICOM	Caribbean Common Market.
CBI	Cross-Border Initiative.
CEMAC	Communauté Économique et Monétaire de l'Afrique Centrale.
CGDC	Consultative Group on Development Co-operation, successor of the CGLC.
CGLC	Consultative Group on Lomé Convention; predecessor of the CGDC.
COMESA	Common Market for Eastern and Southern African States (successor organisation of the PTA).
CMA	Common Monetary Area.
Commission	Commission of the European Union, unless otherwise specified.
CREDIT	Centre for Research in Economic Development and International Trade (of the School of Economics, Nottingham University).
CU	Customs Union.
DRC	Democratic Republic of Congo.
EAC	1. East African Community (successor organisation of the EAHC which broke up in 1977 and currently due for re-launch to replace the East African Co-operation).
	2. East African Co-operation (initiated in 1993 and to be transformed into an East African Community).
EAHC	East African High Commission.
EACM	East African Common Market, also referred to as East African Community (EAC).
ECDPM	European Centre for Development Policy Management.
ECOWAS	Economic Community for West African States.
EDF	European Development Fund.
EIB	European Investment Bank.
EPA	Economic Partnership Agreement.
EU	European Union.

ERO	European Research Office.
FDI	Foreign Direct Investments.
FES	Friedrich-Ebert-Stiftung.
FTA	Free Trade Arrangement.
GATS	General Agreement on Trade and Services
GATT	General Agreements on Trade and Tariff (predecessor to and now part of the WTO).
GDs	General Directorates (proposed for the ACP secretariat).
GDP	Gross Domestic Product.
GLR	Great Lakes Region.
Horn	Horn of Africa (Djibouti, Ethiopia, Eritrea, Somalia).
IBRD	International Bank for Reconstruction and Development (also known as the World Bank).
IDIL	Imani Development (International) Limited.
IDS	Institute of Development Studies, University of Sussex.
IGAD	Intergovernmental Authority on Development.
IIT	Intra-industry trade.
IMF	International Monetary Fund.
IOC	Indian Ocean Commission.
IORARC	Indian Ocean Rim Association for Regional Cooperation.
LC	Lomé Convention.
LDC	Less Developed Country (developing country).
LLDC	Least Developed Country.
MERCOSUR	Mercado Común del Sur (the Common Market of the South American States).
MEP	Member of European Parliament.
MFN	Most Favoured Nation.
NAFTA	North American Free Trade Area.
NEI	Netherlands Economics Institute.
NIP	National Indicative Programme (of the LC).
PACIFIC	Pacific ACP states (Fiji, Kiribati, Tonga, Papua New Guinea, Samoa, Solomon Islands, Tuvalu, and Vanuatu).
PTA	Preferential Trade Area for Eastern and Southern African States (predecessor organisation of COMESA).
RIP	Regional Indicative Programme (of the LC).
RD	Regional Directorate (proposed for the ACP secretariat).
REPA	Regional Economic Partnership Agreement.

ROW	Rest of the World.
RSA	Republic of South Africa (used interchangeably with South Africa).
SACU	Southern African Customs Union.
SADCC	Southern African Development Co-ordination Conference (predecessor of the SADC).
SADC	Southern African Development Community (successor of the SADCC).
SDT	Special and Differential Treatment.
SMEs	Small and Medium-scale enterprises
TBT	Technical Barrier to Trade.
UEMOA	Union Économique et Monétaire Ouest-Africaine.
UNCTAD	United Nations Conference on Trade and Development.
UNIDO	United Nations Industrial Development Organisation.
WEED	World Economy, Ecology and Development
WIPO	World Intellectual Property Organisation.
WTO	World Trade Organisation (successor of the GATT).

Foreword

After 30 years in Tanzania, the Friedrich-Ebert-Stiftung has refocused its activities in order to foster the democratisation process by broadening participation in the country's economic and political development process. This is in recognition of the fact that the participation of the broad population in the economic development process is an important catalyst for a balanced political system, mutually beneficial to all social groups.

Political Dialogue, which was initiated in 1999, addresses broad-based issues. It is a platform for social discourse that brings together experts from various professions and disciplines who can be seen as leaders and opinion makers. In this way it seeks to facilitate constructive dialogue concerning developments in the local and international spheres of significance for national development.

Among other things, the *Political Dialogue* forum brings face to face the diverging positions with regard to the tackling of societal problems and, through constructive discourse, it aims at easing controversies and building consensus.

The deliberations of the various *Political Dialogues* are published at irregular intervals and disseminated to political decision-makers (such as those in parliament and government) and other interested stakeholders in society.

The editor of the *Political Dialogue Series* is Dr. Francis A.S.T. Matambalya, a former scholar of the Friedrich-Ebert-Foundation (FES) who has maintained a long-standing working partnership with the institution. Dr. Matambalya is deeply engaged in both South-South and North-South dialogue, notably through his academic and research endeavours. Currently, he is a Humboldt Scholar and Senior Research Fellow at the Center for Development Research (ZEF) of Bonn University in Germany, directing an international collaborative study on the Small and Medium Scale Enterprises (SMEs) Sector in the economies of the East African Community (EAC).

Our deep gratitude to Mrs Kate Girvan for her tireless support in the proof reading of this production.

Finally, in order to facilitate a real broad-based and critical dialogue, we would highly appreciate feedback in terms of comments from readers. Such comments and suggestions can be addressed directly to FES or to the series editor by normal mail or

Friedrich-Ebert-Stiftung
Peter Haeussler
Resident Director
397 Kawawa Road
P.O. Box 4472, Dar es salaam Tanzania.
fes@fes-tz.org

Dr. Francis A.S.T. Matambalya
Walter-Flex-Strasse 3
D - 53113 Bonn
Germany.
f.matambalya@uni-bonn.de
Bnyangira@hotmail.com

Preface

The negotiations for the renewal of the partnership between the EU and the ACP States began on 30 September 1998 in the wake of two years of public debate on the prospects for the "post-Lomé" period. On 3 February 2000, after eighteen months of in-depth negotiations, the ACP group of nations (currently 77 developing countries, 39 of which are among the least developed) and the EU states concluded a new *Partnership Agreement*. The agreement was signed in Cotonou, the Capital of Gabon on 23 June 2000, and it is scheduled to govern EU-ACP co-operation in the next 20 years.

The ideas presented in this study emanate from a critical observation of the dynamics of EU development policy and the pertinent developments in the international system. The author assesses the viability of and the practical options for regionalised co-operation between the EU and the economies of the Eastern and Southern African sub-region as envisaged in the framework agreement. Through a profound explication of the Lomé Convention (LC) and the pertinent global developments, the author examines the implications of regionalising EU-ACP co-operation for the Eastern and Southern African states within a broader context.

Based on the analysis, he comes out with concrete suggestions on how, in detail, the future co-operation between the EU and its associates from Eastern and Southern African sub-region can be shaped. He makes concrete suggestions on such contentious issues as the scope and geography of co-operation, the modality of linkages, the functionality of ties, and strategic considerations for competitiveness. He proposes co-operation on a broadly-based regional integration scheme with an option for variable geometry. Also, in recognition of the essence of regional integration, he presents an *à la carte* menu of integration schemes, from which the economies of the sub-region can select a base for their co-operation with the EU. According to the author, an equally important issue that the EU should consider in its future development policy is the need to uphold the ACP as a group through a strategy of multi-tierism.

On the whole, the author advocates a general shift in the focus of EU-ACP co-operation towards arrangements that will foster interactions capable of creating and sustaining the competitiveness of the ACP economies in the trade and investment spheres.

The study was proposed by the author and funded by the FES offices in Dar es Salaam and Brussels. It involved, among other things, consultations with various stakeholders in Brussels and in Eastern and Southern Africa. Its initial findings were discussed for the first time in a second *policy dialogue* in May 1999, which was jointly organised by FES and a group of independent Tanzanian stakeholders (comprising researchers, technocrats, academicians, civil society and private sector representatives) who work under the synonym of the Consultative Group on Lomé Convention (CGLC).[1] In the meantime, the study has been comprehensively updated and extended to incorporate the pertinent new developments between May

---

[1] In order to more correctly reflect the nature of its activities, the CGLC has been succeeded by the Consultative Group on Development Co-operation (CGDC).

1999 and the signing of the Cotonou Agreement in June 2000. Part II, which is a completely new addition to the study, has been adapted from the paper "The New EU-ACP Partnership: Making the WTO Lomé Compatible and Vice Versa". This paper was presented by the author at the Expert Meeting "The New EU-ACP Partnership: The Trade Chapter" organised by INZET 17 - 18 April 2000 in Amsterdam, the Netherlands. It also draws from the paper "The Cotonou Agreement and the Challenges of making it WTO Compatible", a forthcoming joint publication by the author and Dr. Susanna Wolf (also a Senior Research Fellow and trade expert at the Center for Development Research of Bonn University) in the *Journal of World Trade* (Vol. No. 34).

While conducting the study, the author had the opportunity to hold discussions with leading experts from both the EU side (DG VIII and European Parliament, officials of selected country and regional missions to the EU and other experts) and the ACP side (officials of selected ACP missions to the EU, ACP Secretariat and the Caribbean Regional Negotiating Machinery) on the development policy of the EU in general and the LC in particular. In this regard, discussions were held with a cross-section of experts from the spheres of research, policy-making and implementation as well as with other stakeholders. The author would like to thank them all for their invaluable remarks. Special gratitude is extended to Mr. Dieter Frisch, former Director General of DG VIII, Mr. Patrick Brandt of the Netherlands Mission in Brussels, and Mr. John Corrie, Member of European Parliament (MEP) and Joint ACP-EU Assembly, Mr. Peter Magande, former Secretary General of the Secretariat of the ACP Group of Nations in Brussels, Dr. Carl Greenidge, former Deputy Secretary General of the Secretariat of the ACP Group of Nations in Brussels and Mr. Peter Gakunu, Chief of the Trade and Customs Division in the ACP Secretariat in Brussels.

Thanks are also due to all those who participated in the second policy dialogue, jointly organised by FES and CGLC in Dar es Salaam on 31 May 1999 where the original version of this study was presented. Moreover, the author benefited from constructive criticism proffered by Dr. Susanna Wolf of the Center for Development Research (Bonn University) and Mr. Walter Kennes of the Commission of the European Union. Their comments were crucial in improving the quality of the study.

The views presented in this study strictly reflect the author's own opinion and do not mirror the official policy of the institutions to which either the author or any discussion partner is affiliated.

Dr. Francis A.S.T. Matambalya
Series Editor
2000

Bonn, June

I BACKGROUND ISSUES

1. Introduction
1.1. EU-ACP development co-operation on the road to change

Relatively recent changes in the international system have heralded a turning point in international alliances. Some of the important dimensions of these changes since 1989 include the *de facto* demise of the "hard approach" to communism and the end of the cold war, the conclusion of the *Uruguay round of negotiations* and the establishment of the World Trade Organisation (WTO) in 1995 following the Marrakech Agreement of 1993, and the proliferation of the bloc-building process in many regions of the world. One of the outcomes is the increasing conflict between multilateralism and regionalism (van Dijk 2000).

The status of EU-ACP co-operation in particular has been influenced by the deepening of the integration process in the EU through the Maastricht Treaty and the east- and northward expansion of the EU through the accession of Austria, Finland and Sweden. Finally, wavering confidence in the LC because of its limited achievements is a major reason for considering a reform of the convention (Matambalya 1999a and 1997, Matambalya 1998, Solignac-Lecomte 1998).

With this background, negotiations for a successor arrangement to the Lomé IV began in the last quarter of 1998. The negotiations were scheduled to be concluded in February 2000 and were primarily about a *Framework Agreement* of principles on which a successor regime to Lomé IV would be built, and the interim arrangement that would apply before a new convention came into force.

From the outset the negotiating mandates of the EU and ACP states revealed agreement on many basic issues and also areas of contention. Overall, the ACP position strongly emphasised the need to uphold the *status quo*, keeping as much of the LC preferences as possible and even enhancing them. The EU position, on the other hand, was for radical changes. Pessimists feared that, if implemented in their full range, the EU proposals would effectively put an end to the Lomé era. With these significantly contradictory positions, the negotiations began in Brussels on 30 September 1998 (EU 1998, ACP 1998, MacQueen 1999, Matambalya 1999b).

The negotiations went through critical moments with the feeling that they were heading towards a dead end. However, towards the end there were signs of readiness for concessions from both sides. The ACP states acknowledged the need for major changes to the LC as a model of development co-operation, while the EU acknowledged the need to uphold the special linkages to its ACP associates.

In the light of the recently signed *Framework Agreement*, this study looks closely at a major feature of the new partnership, i.e., the regionalisation of EU-ACP linkages. It explores the possibility of accommodating both the ACP and EU interests within the detailed negotiations that will follow the *Framework Agreement*. It builds on the argument that, in such an arrangement, *multi-tierism* can provide a plausible option which will help to ease *consensus* between the EU and its ACP associates, while at the same time opening the vent for the exploitation of the obvious advantages of the regionalisation of EU-ACP co-operation.

The study focuses in particular on the Eastern and Southern African ACP States. By and large the region's states conform to the member states of the three major integration schemes in the grand sub-region of Africa south of the Sahara, i.e., the Southern African Development Community (SADC), the East African Community (EAC), and the Indian Ocean Commission (IOC).[2] The area also covers the Southern African Customs Union (SACU).

1.2. Preliminary reflections on post-Lomé EU-ACP development co-operation

The initial reflections on the future of EU-ACP co-operation were gloomy. Due to the overwhelming scepticism surrounding the achievements of the LC, and to the erosion of the geopolitical significance of the ACP after the collapse of communism, need for change was imminent. In tandem with the pressure for change, it was feared that the dissolution of the convention was inevitable and impending.

Eventually the Commission's *Green Paper* (EU 1996) suggested major changes and implied the EU's preference for a departure from the Lomé culture, thereby sparking further ACP fears regarding the intentions of the EU. Following the publication of the *Green Paper*, it dawned upon the ACP states that concerted efforts were necessary to salvage this important arrangement for their economies. This was clearly documented in the Libreville Agreement and subsequent position documents of the ACP group including its negotiating mandate. Making reference to, *inter alia*, the continued absence of *a level playing field*, the ACP group reminded the EU of the unbearable burden to the ACP economies of sweeping liberalisation, and expressed hope that the international community would understand its concerns (ACP 1998, ACP 1997).

1.3. Aim and structure of the study

In technical jargon, the *Framework Agreement* presents an *agreement in principle* (as opposed to an *agreement on details*) on the modalities for co-operation. Concretely, this means that it broadly sketches the intentions and outlines the skeleton of co-operation, without attending to the pertinent details. Therefore, at this stage, the really sticky issues related to the details of the co-operation, remain untouched. In this study, we make preliminary deliberations as a contribution to the impending detailed negotiations scheduled to begin in September 2002, as laid down in Article 37 of the *Framework Agreement*.

The study is divided into five major parts. Part I briefly looks at the background issues preceding the *Framework Agreement*, including the proposals for "Regional Economic Partnership Agreements" (REPAs). Part II highlights the *Framework Agreement* including the "Economic Partnership Agreement" (EPA) model of

---

[2] Of course, the Common Market for Eastern and Southern Africa (COMESA) constitutes a further major integration initiative with many members from Eastern and Southern Africa. However, we have deliberately selected not to base our discussion on it for two major reasons:
- The co-operation agenda of COMESA is rather narrowly defined and confined to trade, while in this paper we deal with all aspects of development.
- As an integration scheme, the COMESA has a stronger pan-africanist orientation. For instance, it includes such countries as Egypt, Sudan, etc., which lie far afield from the sample region of this study (i.e., Eastern and Southern Africa).

development co-operation. Part III dwells on the key issues which should be addressed by the Eastern and Southern African States in the work of post-Lomé IV EU-ACP development co-operation in the area of trade and beyond. Part IV contains recommendations and concluding remarks, while appendixes are presented in part V.

2. *EU's proposal to regionalise its co-operation with its ACP associates*

The cornerstone of the initial proposal by the EU to reform the post-Lomé IV development co-operation model was the regionalisation of EU-ACP linkages. Thus, the resulting debate centred on ACP regions and, in the case of Africa, sub-regions as the loci for development co-operation. While explicitly meaning *regionalised arrangements*, it also implied prospects for *multi-tierism*.

In addition, the EU's proposal stressed trade reciprocity in compliance with multi-lateralism. Therefore, the proposed reforms constituted a call for a major shift from the Lomé culture with respect to three important dimensions, i.e., the locus of development co-operation, the disposition of differential treatment, and the conceptual base of the model of development co-operation.

2.1. Technical implications of regionalising EU-ACP co-operation
2.1.1. Shift of the loci of EU-ACP development co-operation

All along it has been known that, despite many similarities, Africa, the Caribbean and the Pacific are distinct regions in the ACP group of states and differ significantly. In Africa, the biggest of the three ACP regions, the differences among the sub-regions are also significant. In order to take these differences into consideration the regionalisation of EU-ACP linkages therefore formed the cornerstone of the EU's proposed post-Lomé IV development co-operation model. In this model, the regions (and sub-regions) were to assume the role of the loci of co-operation.

Subsequently, it was assumed that the selection of regions (and in the case of Africa, sub-regions) for the REPA studies indicated the EU's preference for a geographical configuration of the ACP regions and sub-regions modelled on regionalisation schemes which already exist (or can be started) in the African, the Caribbean and the Pacific regions.[3] In this regard, the "regions" that constituted serious potential partners of the EU in a future model of development co-operation included the EAC, the IOC, the SADC and the SACU.[4]

---

[3] Notably, for a simulation of the impact on ACP economies of the introduction of reciprocity in its trade with the ACP states, six ACP sub-regions/regions were selected. They included four existing regionalisation schemes in Africa (i.e., CEMAC, EAC, SADC and UEMOA, which also covers Ghana), and one existing regionalisation scheme in the Caribbean (i.e., CARICOM, which also covers the Dominican Republic). The Pacific states were taken as one region mainly because no regionalisation scheme exists in the area as yet.

[4] Though not included in the REPA research the COMESA is also important for the Southern African

2.1.2. Asymmetrical liberalisation and differential treatment

Asymmetrical liberalisation (i.e., the EU liberalising faster and more comprehensively than the ACP states) and differentiation formed two further major issues in the proposed post-Lomé IV agenda for development co-operation.

Through *asymmetrical liberalisation*[5], the EU was going to liberalise faster and more comprehensively, while the ACP states were to liberalise systematically (using a transition phase of at least 10 years as per WTO provisions) and "less" comprehensively than the EU. Hence, the ACP economies would have not been required to liberalise the importation of the more sensitive products until 2010 or thereafter.

In general terms, it meant that EU co-operation with various ACP regions and sub-regions would centre on regionally differentiated programmes of action according to such criteria as, location, level of development, unique regional needs and past performance.

Also, though the regions and sub-regions were expected to form the loci of co-operation, differentiation could be applied between two countries from the same region (e.g., between a least developed country and one which is not), depending on their level of development.

2.2. Conceptual base of regionalised co-operation: trade-driven co-operation

In technical terms, the EU proposed the establishment of the so-called "Regional Economic Partnership Agreements" (REPAs). In conventional economic terms, a REPA is a model of development co-operation built around trade liberalisation. Hence, the core of this model is the creation of free trade areas (FTAs). Consequently, pro-REPA arguments draw mainly on the conventional gains of market integration, where liberalisation brings gains of *static welfare nature* and *dynamic nature*.

The key characterising features of REPAs as envisaged in the original proposal could then be generalised as follows (UNIDO 1999: 17, Matambalya 1999c: 4, Matambalya 1999f, Stevens 1999):

(a) The non-LLDCs were to reciprocate EU preferences. Technically, this means the reduction or removal of tariffs on most imports from the EU.

(b) Initially it was envisaged that REPAs should apply primarily to merchandise trade, while trade in services was to remain subject to "most favoured nation"

States as it draws most of its members from the region.

[5] The *asymmetry* refers to two aspects: (i) the timing of tariff phase down (i.e., one partner, who in this case is the EU, will reduce and eliminate its tariffs faster than the other partners, who in this case is the ACP region or sub-region) and (ii) the extent of total trade included in tariff reduction and tariff elimination under the REPA (meaning that one partner, who in this case is the EU, will reduce and eliminate tariffs on a higher percentage of its total trade than the other partners, who is in this case the ACP region or sub-region).

status (MFN) in accordance with the WTO provisions. However, during the debate, movement was discernible in this integral aspect of the initial proposal. It became increasingly clear that the adopted agreement was likely to include co-operation in trade in services, as well as in trade-related issues.

(c) The implementation of REPAs was to run parallel to negotiations for the further liberalisation of global trade within the multi-lateral fora. Hence, it became clear that members of the "Rest of the World" (ROW) could pressurise the EU and ACP states to generalise the liberalisation they extend to each other, making them accessible to other trade partners as well.

One of the key merits of a REPA was that, as an FTA, it could be justified internationally within the framework of multilateral trade arrangements.

2.3. Postulated arguments for REPAs

To understand at least the short-term economic impact of introducing sweeping reciprocity into EU-ACP trade, among other things we have to:

(a) Adopt a framework of analysis comparing two "blocs" of nations with *dissimilar levels of productivity* and *different social economic systems*.[6] In this regard, effective integration modelled upon a REPA depends on the state of economic structure[7] (e.g., industrial structure) of the ACP regions and sub-regions. Some of the inevitable questions in this connection are: Do the ACP economies have industry compatible with industry in the EU? Are there prospects for significant intra-industry trade (IIT) or intra-company trade between the EU and the ACP?

(b) Consider the extent to which the existing economic constellations will generate dynamic gains. Hence, we have to put into perspective the *dynamic aspects* of integration, to reflect how the EU and its ACP associates can through REPAs, coalesce to give the right signals to the economic actors. Those signals should, in turn, guide shifts in the pattern of investments and production.

(c) Consider also the *static aspects* of integration, including their possible scope and certainty. An inevitable consideration here is the security of any static welfare gains against erosion.

In accordance with integration theory, liberalisation may result in *static welfare gains* and *dynamics gains*. Concretely, the former will be due to *price advantages*, and the latter will result from *shifts in investment and production*. In addition to these conventional gains of integration, the merging of high performance and low

---

[6] In this context, we have to relate *investment to output, output to productivity,* and *productivity to prices*. Likewise interesting are the relations of *productivity to wages, and wages to employment and incomes*. Within a broader context, we may also relate *productivity to the prices of all other factors of production*.

[7] Notably, if the ACP country, region or sub-region concluding a REPA with the EU is essentially an exporter of raw materials, the chances are that the "North-South" integration a la REPA will be relatively meaningless.

performance areas is associated with dynamic gains related to *lock-in effects*[8,] and in terms of *upward convergence*[9] (IDIL 1998, Matambàlya 1999c, Whiting 1993).

2.3.1. Static welfare gains

The welfare effects, as used in this context, express a component of *competition effect* of REPA. Arguably, inasmuch as a REPA can increase competition (for domestic producers and for other suppliers) on the domestic ACP markets, it is likely to trigger lower prices, due to either *trade creation* or *trade diversion*. Trade creation refers to the extra trade generated by the reduction or complete removal of the tariffs on goods imported from the EU. This will be the result if the more efficient EU suppliers replace the less efficient ACP suppliers. However, this will also depend on the degree of substitutability of locally produced and imported goods.

By the same token, trade diversion refers to the extent to which ACP imports will substitute suppliers from the ROW against suppliers for whom tariffs have fallen relatively. Concretely, this means, the magnitude by which import supply will be diverted from the ROW to the EU, in the aftermath of the reduction or complete removal of tariffs, in line with the trade regime of the new EU-ACP co-operation agreement.

In any event, in nominal terms, the postulated welfare gains are predicated upon *price advantages* associated with liberalisation (UNIDO 1999, IDIL 1998, Matambalya 1999c). The main beneficiaries will be the final consumers and the ACP consumers of intermediate products and machinery imported from the EU.

2.3.2. Dynamic gains

The envisaged dynamic effects underscore the *competition effect* of a REPA as well. In line with integration economics, they are attributed to investment and production shifts. Expressed in simple terms, we will reap dynamic gains if trade liberalisation generates significantly increased levels of investment. Hence, one of the basic dynamic aspects of a REPA is that trade liberalisation eventually creates a conducive, more stable and more inviting investment environment in the respective ACP country, region or sub-region. Subsequently, liberalisation is expected to enhance investor confidence, thereby triggering more investments, partly due to assured market access and the posited *lock-in effect*.

---

[8] The *lock-in effect*, in this context, denotes the expected sustainability of liberalisation (i.e., tariff reductions) and other economic reforms. The logic behind this is that reforms in the ACP regions and sub-regions can be sustained, if there is enhanced co-operation with the EU, in which case the latter will play the role of the "agency for restraint". In this way, the credibility of trade reforms, macroeconomic reforms and the legal framework will be enhanced (ECDPM 1998a: 2-3, Matambalya 1999c: 6).

[9] The upward convergence means that those starting at the low end systematically move up towards those at the high end, in such a way that the ones at the high end do not go down (Reynolds 1993).

However, it has to be borne in mind, as pointed out above, the realisation of dynamic aspects depends on whether the EU and its ACP associates can coalesce to give the right signals to shifts in the pattern of investments and production.[10]

Also, increased investments will trigger a range of other dynamic benefits associated with upward convergence. In an optimistic scenario, as investments increase and EU-ACP integration deepens, there will be a systematic *upward convergence of levels of income* in the ACP countries, regions and sub-regions, which will help to alleviate poverty.[11]

Furthermore, the ACP economies will benefit from competitive economic restructuring which in the long run will facilitate their integration into the world economy as credible competitors in industrial production and trade. In an ideal political scenario, this will result from, *inter alia*, the upward convergence of productivity (Cohen 1993, Whiting Jr. 1993).[12]

Besides equalisation in levels of income, further equalisation in terms of upward convergence may be associated with environmental standards, i.e., through deeper links with the EU, the ACP economies will benefit from a systematic *upward convergence of environmental standards*.[13]

Arguably also, to the extent that REPAs will foster regional integration, one of the most important dynamic gains that can be associated with them are the *resultant improved growth rates* of the economies of the ACP regions and sub-regions.[14]

2.4. Postulated arguments against REPAs
2.4.1. Potential costs of REPAs

To the extent that a REPA between the EU and its ACP associates involves merging developed (high performance) and developing (low performance) economies, it will also generate differential cost burdens. Integration economic theory can help us trace the trend of development of these costs.[15] Therefore, overall,

---

[10] Imperatively, the much quoted *lock-in effect* of REPAs can only be attained in the real sense, if the EU and ACP economies will blend their production dynamics in a way that fosters mutually beneficial *substitutability* and *complementariness* between domestic and foreign investments in the ACP region.

[11] This will also be technically possible, in accordance with the axiom of *factor price equalisation*, which by experience constitutes a dynamic gain ascribed to deeper integration between high performance and low performance economies (Minford 1998, Cohen 1993, Reynolds 1993).

[12] Overall, this will also be in line with two key theories, i.e., *industrial organisation and locational theory*, and the *theory of globalisation of industry*.

[13] Environmental standards are crucial because they affect the costs of the factors of production.

[14] The argument partly derives from the observation of a strong correlation between the growth in exports of manufactured goods and the growth rates of gross domestic product (GDP) (Buitelaar 1993).

[15] Analogous to the arguments for the benefits of a REPA, in order to understand the economic impact of introducing reciprocity in EU-ACP trade, we have to consider the differences in the levels of development. Notably, we are dealing with a situation of merging two "blocs" of nations with *dis-*

there will be unfavourable shifts in revenue structures, heralded by losses in government revenues due to foregone customs revenues, and economic restructuring.

Concretely, these costs can be divided into *fiscal costs, adjustment costs*, and *losses due to negative dynamic effects* (of shifts) *in the domestic production and investment base*. The REPA study for the SADC, for instance, estimates an *overall balance of losses* (i.e., the combined shifts in consumer gains and revenue structures) ranging from 27.9 percent to 0.4 percent for the SADC economies (IDIL 1998: 117, Matambalya 1999c: 10).

A. Fiscal effects of liberalisation

The fiscal effects of liberalisation refer to the impact of liberalisation on government revenues. Accordingly, the foregone customs revenues herald losses in government revenue, particularly in the absence of appropriate measures to develop alternative sources of revenues (Matambalya 1999c, ERO 1998). To highlight, the two REPA studies commissioned by the EU, covering two integration schemes in the region (i.e., EAC and SADC) implied massive losses of revenues for the ACP economies.[16]

Taking 1996 as the base year and assuming also that the SADC economies apply a general 30 percent reduction from the current MFN tariff rates by the year 2015, the relevant impact study made key observations regarding the impact on *customs revenues, welfare, added value of a REPA*.[17] Hence, in the event of establishing a REPA modelled on the proposed assumptions:

(a) At 70 percent, 27.9 percent, 30 percent, 23 percent, 22 percent for Seychelles, Mauritius, Tanzania, Mozambique, and Zambia, respectively, and between 0.8 and 6.3 percent for the remaining countries, the losses in customs revenues will be significant (IDIL 1998: 117, Matambalya 199c:10).

(b) For 11 of the 14 SADC economies, the welfare gains will not exceed 0.5 millions of US dollars (IDIL 1998: 117, Matambalya 199c:10).

(c) Due to reduced preferences, the SADC economies will experience losses with respect to *value of access* to the EU market under REPA terms, with the LDCs in the group (i.e., Mauritius and Zimbabwe) suffering over-proportional losses (IDIL 1998).

Likewise, the study for the EAC projected heavy losses in tariff and tax revenues, due to duty-free imports from the EU. Accordingly, expressed relative to 1995:

---

similar levels of productivity and *different social economic systems*. The complementary dynamics of such an integration process are likely to differ significantly from those of an integration involving economies at, by and large, similar levels of economic development and comparable socio-economic systems.

[16] Note that a second round of studies on the impact of introducing reciprocity into EU-ACP trade, commissioned by the Secretariat of the ACP Group of nations, though using different methodology came to, by and large, similar conclusions.

[17] The *value added* is computed as the difference between *value of access* (i.e., duty-free access for LLDCs and improved GSP for LDCs in the EU market, against EU improved MFN rates) *and value of access REPA* (based on assumptions of duty-free access of all SADC exports to the EU, against EU improved MFN rates) (IDIL 1998: 112, Matambalya 1999c: 10).

(a) Kenya will experience losses of tax revenues amounting to 82 percent, and total losses of tax revenues of 12 percent (CREDIT, 1998: 11).

(b) Tanzania will experience losses of tax revenues in the tune of 73 percent, and total losses of tax revenues of 20 percent, (CREDIT 1998: 11).

(c) Uganda will experience losses of tax revenues equivalent to 69 percent, and total losses of tax revenues of 16 percent (CREDIT 1998: 11).

In the foreseeable future the erosion of the revenue bases for the governments is likely to trigger a chain reaction of negative events, manifested in the inability of governments to perform their functions. Among other things:

(a) The level and quality of public services (e.g., education, health care, etc.) will drop further. In countries like Tanzania, where financial distress has already rendered these services destitute, the situation may change from emergency to catastrophic proportions.

(b) Debt-related hardships will be aggravated, as even higher shares of total government revenues are directed at debt servicing.

(c) Extensive retrenchments at all levels may become inevitable, devastating further the government machinery, since wages constitute a significant share of government expenditure in developing countries. Notably, wages averaged 35.5 percent for the period 1984 to 1990 for Swaziland. Even for such a relatively richer SADC economy, as Zimbabwe, the comparable figure was 28.4 percent (Matambalya 1999b: 211, Matambalya 1997: 209).

B. Adjustment costs of liberalisation

Typically, adjustment costs arise from *reduced competitiveness* and *reliance on tariff revenues*. It is evident that the economies of the region rely on tariff revenues. For instance, about 33.3 percent of government revenue in Tanzania is derived from import duties. In the case of Uganda, revenues from internationally traded goods account for about 60 percent of total tax revenue (IDIL 1998, CREDIT 1998: 10, UNIDO 1999: 18).

Adjustment costs due to reduced competitiveness arise when tariffs are eliminated or reduced, so that formerly protected industries find themselves in a more competitive environment (and are unable to compete with imports). Whether the competitiveness of the EU will be due *to cost efficiency* (and trade creation) or domestic *subsidies* (and possibly trade diversion) is, at this point of the analysis, irrelevant.[18] More important is the fact that the resultant losses may compel closures by the less competitive ACP producers, and cause the general reduction of economic activity. Overall, adjustment costs of this nature will also aggravate further the problem of unemployment (ERO 1998, Matambalya 1999c).

---

[18] The extent to which REPAs increase competition on the domestic market of the liberalising economy (through trade creation or diversion/deflection) depends on the extent to which tariff cuts are passed on to the purchasers in the form of lower prices.

Related to this, there will be *adjustment costs* attributable to such factors as the re-allocation of resources from the ACP producers "displaced" by lower-cost imports from the EU, economic restructuring, the costs of the development of alternative sources of revenue, etc.

The severity of the adjustment costs of liberalisation will depend on the extent to which the *pace* and *degree* of tariff reduction and elimination exceeds the ability of domestic industries to improve their efficiency.

C. Erosion of static welfare gains

ACP governments left with no revenue basis as a result of liberalisation are likely to raise sales taxes and other taxes tied to consumption as alternative sources to customs revenues. This will in effect reduce the margin of price advantage caused by, for instance, trade creation. Hence, changes in domestic tax regimes will, *ipso facto*, erode the static welfare gains from ACP purchasers of imports from the EU.

Notably, the costs in this group can be seen as part of the adjustment costs, since they arise concomitant with the government's efforts to develop alternative sources of revenue. However, considering their importance, it is probably correct to highlight them separately.

D. Negative dynamic effects of liberalisation on domestic production

Negative dynamic effects also denote a competitive aspect of liberalisation. Within this context, losses (or negative dynamic effects) are likely to be associated with *shifts in domestic investment and production base*. A typical shift in this regard will be the *crowding out of* (the less efficient) *domestic investments*, due to the entry into the market of more efficient EU investors keen on utilising the economies of scale and other advantages offered by the liberalised ACP regional markets. The initial typical market reactions may be exacerbated by the vulnerability of the ACP producers to EU subsidies, which may force economic restructuring in the concerned ACP economies. Losses triggered in this way may also lead to closures by the less competitive ACP producers, which in turn exacerbate unemployment (Matambalya 1999c).

A more complex and pessimistic scenario involves the likely enhancement of one-sided dependence of the ACP economies on the EU. Notably, an FTA that will discriminate the ROW against the EU may lead to two developments. First, the more efficient EU counterparts will push the less efficient ACP investors out of the market. Second, enterprises from ROW will continue to face higher market entry barriers on the ACP markets, compared to their EU competitors. Thus, the EU investors will capitalise on their comparative advantage, and utilise the economies of scale to consolidate even further their positions on the ACP markets.[19]

Also, a REPA may affect the ACP economies through the *diversion of* (discriminated) *investments* from the ROW. This is a likely scenario, where discrimination (of access of ROW products into ACP markets) will be compounded by *rule of origin* regarding the entry of ACP products into the EU.

---

[19] This explains in part, claims of "mercantilist motives" behind the EU's REPA proposal (Matambalya 1999c, McQueen 1998).

2.4.2. Contentious issues regarding REPAs

A. Status of the ACP group

As part of their resolution to maintain the *status quo*, the ACP states reiterated on several occasions their desire to remain together as a single unit. This position was not always explicitly shared by the EU, which both in the *Green Paper* and also in its REPA proposals suggested a regional differentiation of co-operation. It remained silent on the prospect of maintaining the ACP as a group (e.g., through multi-tierism involving a global arrangement and besides regional arrangements). This caused anxiety in the ACP group.

B. "Geography of regionalisation"

Right from the start, it was clear that the EU strongly believes in the virtue of regionalisation as a model of development, and in its own capacity to promote regionalisation, given its vast experience in regional integration. Hence, for the EU, REPAs with ACP regions or sub-regions constituted a preferable proposal, though a vent was also left open for bilateral arrangements with individual countries. The simulated REPA studies for instance, covered the Caribbean states as one group, the Pacific states as another group, and four regionalisation schemes in Africa.

Implicitly, there are basic problems with this "regionalisation" approach:

(a) In Africa, the identified regional organisations did not comprehensively cover all ACP economies. Concretely, they excluded 17 LLDCs (i.e., Burundi, Cape Verde, Comoros, Djibouti, Eritrea, Ethiopia, Gambia, Guinea, Guinea Bissau, Liberia, Madagascar, Mauritania, Rwanda, Sao Tomé and Prince Pe, Sierra Leone, Somalia, and Sudan), and 2 LDCs (i.e., Ghana and Nigeria).

(b) Some countries, like Tanzania (a member of both EAC and SADC), belong to more than one major integration schemes, defined as a potential partner of the EU in a REPA.

(c) The REPA offered the LLDCs a non-reciprocal Lomé parity, which could woo them away from their regional alliances.

(d) The requirement for LDCs in a region to liberalise with regard to EU imports while the LLDCs should not, also contradicts the efforts to promote regional integration.

Another serious problem is the lack of clarity on who was mandated to determine the geographical demarcation of a region or a sub-region. Although the EU insisted that the terms of reference do not represent its thinking for the geography of REPAs, there was room for wrong assumptions. This situation was another source of uncertainty for the ACP member countries.

C. Compliance with multilateralism

In this regard, it was argued that FTAs could be based on Article XXIV of the GATT on Customs Unions and Free Trade Areas (revised in 1994), the Enabling Clause on special and differential treatment, and Article IX of the 1994 Marrakech Agreement, (formerly Article XXV of the GATT) (UNIDO 1999: 16).

However, this did not eliminate the ambiguity surrounding the issue, and despite these provisions, the WTO conformity of an FTA between the EU and its ACP associates remained nebulous for a number of reasons:

(a) Regarding liberalisation by the EU, it was not clear whether "substantially all trade" would be compatible with the Common Agricultural Policy (CAP), which protects certain EU products.

(b) As regards WTO's interpretation of "substantially all trade", it was noted by critical observers that there is no special provision for liberalisation schemes involving both LDCs and LLDCs, while all potential ACP regions and sub-regions for a REPA contain both LDCs and LLDCs (ECDPM 1998).[20]

(c) Whether a waiver to back the special EU-ACP relations was going to be obtained from the WTO and the duration of an eventual such waiver are issues that could not be taken for granted.

D. Ambiguity surrounding differentiation

The *open-ended* character of the differentiation provision of the REPA concept, while meant to express EU flexibility and goodwill, could in practice have a negative rather than positive impact. Inasmuch as it pursues sometimes *conflicting goals* of *regional differentiation* (i.e., grouping ACP economies into regions and sub-regions) and *differentiation according to the level of development* (i.e., categorising ACP economies in LLDCs and LDCs), it gives an ambiguous message to the ACP economies. Therefore, it contains an intrinsic danger of de-linking some countries from the integration schemes, thereby impeding, instead of fostering, regional integration (Goodison 1998, Matambalya 1999a, Stevens 1999).

E. Uncertainties regarding the treatment of services

The implicit exclusion of the service sector from preferential treatment may have proven to be costly to ACP states. Among other things, the small island states which heavily rely on trade in services (e.g., from the tourism sector) may have been over-proportionally affected. Also, this stance may have given wrong signals to local investors in countries like Tanzania which are currently striving to develop this sector. Even countries like Kenya, which have a relatively well-developed tourist sector, may have suffered.

However, the softening of EU's position and the indication to include trade in services and co-operation in trade-related issues in the future Convention gave some hope. Yet it remains to be seen how this can be implemented within the framework of extending special treatment to the sector, at least in line with SDT.

---

[20] This means that, if the EU extends special preferences to LLDCs within a given regionalisation scheme having FTA arrangements with the Union, it must technically extend them to all members of the FTA, even non-LLDCs. For Eastern and Southern Africa, they will have to be extended to countries like Botswana, Mauritius, South Africa (if it remains a member of the regionalisation schemes) and Zimbabwe.
Alternatively, if the EU denies the LDCs special treatment, this should apply to the LLDCs as well (ECDPM 1998a).

F. Questionable market-related gains

Under Lomé IV, the EU had already significantly liberalised its market with respect to exports from the ACP economies. Notably, 99.5 percent of ACP's exports to the EU were enjoying duty-free access (Matambalya 1999b, Matambalya 1998, Matambalya 1997). This implies that, even if the 0.5 percent is removed, the effective liberalisation margin (i.e., the real effective impact) on market access, the volume of trade and export revenues for the ACP economies will be insignificant. On the other hand, as a result of trade creation and trade diversion, the introduction of reciprocity into EU-ACP trade will significantly boost market access of EU products on ACP markets.

One way to avert this imbalance would have been to reform the CAP, which, for realistic reasons, is a very sensitive aspect of European politics. This suggests that the EU may have to offer something else in exchange, but what exactly?

G. Institutional requirements for the enforcement of REPAs

From the REPA proposal, it could be discerned that regionalised EU-ACP linkages would need powerful and efficient supranational organisations to oversee their enforcement. However, the indication in the *Green Paper* (EU 1996) of a possible splitting up of the ACP group implicitly put the role of the ACP secretariat into question. Eventually it was implied that it would be necessary to maintain the ACP group together with the secretariat (Corrie 1998). Nonetheless, it was not made clear whether in future the ACP secretariat would solely be responsible for the co-ordination work (i.e., even in the case of regionalised arrangements), or there would be a sharing of responsibilities, with specific roles being delegated to supra-national bodies of the ACP regions and sub-regions. In particular, the apparent role of regional bodies was not addressed.

H. Relevance of the REPA studies

As pointed out by Matambalya (1999: 8-9), though constituting an important contribution to the debate on the future form of co-operation between the EU and its ACP associates, several aspects of the REPA studies themselves could be contested.

First, the studies were *limited in scope*. Thus, though conceptually REPAs represented a development co-operation model that embraces more than "free trade", the studies were, by and large, restricted to trade issues. Their limited scope left gaps and this reduced the utility of the studies in providing the information necessary for making decisions in favour of or against the REPAs.

Second, concerning the *approach and analytical focus*, technically the REPA studies were *ex-ante* studies based on (subjective) assumptions. Implicitly, the results depend on the assumptions. Thus, for the results to have statistical and policy relevance, the assumptions must conform to reality.

Third, to the extent that *dynamic models* might have given more superior results than the *static models* used, the *studies were deficient in their empirical formulations*.

Fourth, even the consultants themselves acknowledged that data was either not readily available or of poor quality (CREDIT 1998, McQueen 1999, etc.).

Fifth, the studies lacked sufficient *analytical depth and base*. The studies were hurriedly done because of the financial and time constraints. In these essentially desk studies, the consultants were compelled to make many simplified assumptions.

Sixth, is the questionable *consistency and relevance of the assumptions*. Notably, in the impact studies contracted by the EU Commission, different assumptions were made by the various teams of consultants, hence reducing their comparability.[21] Furthermore, the studies made severely limiting assumptions. Some of the assumptions made in the EU-commissioned studies were: (i) the perfect substitutability of local goods by imported goods from the EU; (ii) the existence of competition between local goods and goods imported from the EU; (iii) the passing on of tariff reduction to purchasers; (iv) the "automatic" flow of EU and other investments to the ACP regions and sub-regions, as a result of liberalisation a la REPA, etc. An important postulation that is worth mentioning separately here is the projection that the main beneficiaries of liberalisation will be consumers of intermediate products and machinery, which constitute the bulk of imports to many ACP regions and sub-regions from the EU. In a real world situation, the extent to which a REPA would have increased competition in the ACP markets would have depended on the proportion of tariff reduction passed on to the purchasers (i.e., consumers of finished goods, and producers who purchase imported or competing locally produced intermediate goods). Furthermore, only substantial price cuts will increase competition and lead to trade creation.

Seventh, the studies did not adequately articulate the impact on the individual ACP economies of, for instance, both adopting a REPA with some economies, and the application of the *acquis* for others from the same region.

---

[21] Additionally, the basic assumptions made in the EU-commissioned studies and in those which were eventually commissioned by the ACP secretariat are significantly different. This reduces the comparability of the two sets of studies and, to a certain extent, it defeats the meaning of the latter set of studies (i.e., those commissioned be the ACP Secretariat).

II THE FRAMEWORK AGREEMENT: FROM REPAs TO EPAs

3. The framework agreement for EU-ACP co-operation: a brief overview

The ACP and EU's agreement to reform their development co-operation is best appreciated when viewed against the present constellation of the liberalisation of the global economy through the globalisation of industry, multi-lateralism and open regionalism. In principle, through the *Framework Agreement* the parties have reached consensus on the diverse issues broached during the negotiations. Already now, it is obvious that a lot of optimism is tied to the agreement. This is underscored by the hailing of the agreement by both parties. According to the ACP group of nations "*the new Agreement gives fresh impetus to relations between Europe and its partners in Africa, the Caribbean and the Pacific and reflects a shared ambition to take up the challenges of a shifting international scene*" (ACP Group of Nations, Information Memo No. 10).

From the EU side Poul Nielson, the European Commissioner for Development and Humanitarian Aid, described the Agreement as "*a remarkable, innovative achievement which faces up to the challenges of globalisation by setting out an integrated and comprehensive approach to development, poverty eradication, trade and political dialogue. This Agreement represents a major contribution to the effort to create international governance and promote North-South dialogue in the post-Seattle era*" (ACP Group of Nations, Information Memo No. 10).

In general terms, the new Partnership Agreement will enable relations between the ACP Group of Nations and the EU states to continue on a reformed basis. Building on the consensus reached in October 1999, the new agreement, which ushers in the end of the Lomé era, hinges on three interactive pillars: the *political dimension*, the *development strategies* and *economic and trade co-operation*. In this context, the texts of the Agreement include specific undertakings for the EU and ACP states as well as less clearly defined obligations which will need further clarification.

It is blatantly obvious that the *Framework Agreement* also reflects the relative strength of the two parties. The EU, with its pro-active stance, more professional negotiating mechanism, greater negotiating capacity and clearer vision, succeeded in incorporating many of its proposals into the new Agreement.

The discussion in this chapter focuses on the trade regime which falls under the economic and trade co-operation. The key questions which we shall attempt to answer are: will the new arrangements be compatible with the rules of the World Trade Organisation (WTO) or will the WTO rules be made compatible with the post-Lomé agreement? What are the options for tackling incompatibility with WTO global trading rules? Does the WTO need reforms to cater for economic partnership agreements (EPAs) between countries at different levels of development? Within this general context, we shall also highlight the role that can be played by the Enabling Clause, and Article XXIV of the WTO, as well as the position of the non-ACP least developed countries (LLDCs).

3.1 Economic partnership as the basis of development co-operation

As already pointed out above, following the initial proposal in the Green Paper (European Commission 1996), the position later advanced by the EU and which dominated the debate on the reform of the Lomé Convention (LC), was the replacement of Lomé IV by REPAs. By the end of the official EU-ACP negotiations, emphasis had shifted from REPAs to EPAs. However, it is noteworthy that the EPA framework co-operation remains firmly rooted to ideas that were already deliberated under the debate of REPAs. In this regard, among other things, the principal direction of the reform of the trade regime of the LC is towards a trade regime or trade regimes that will introduce reciprocity into EU-ACP trade, as well as being programmed to facilitate progressive transition towards free trade areas (FTAs) between the EU and the ACP counterparts. Such FTAs must comply with the provisions of the WTO.

3.1.1. Theoretical base and practical orientation of the EPA model of development co-operation

Despite the change of terminology from REPAs to EPAs, the framework agreement conspicuously builds on the REPA proposal with respect to, *inter alia*, the regional focus of development co-operation, the theoretical base of the proposed development co-operation model, and the essential features of the co-operation.

A. *Theoretical base of the EPA model of development co-operation*

The envisaged EPAs are *de facto* trade-driven economic co-operation arrangements, in which the concept of FTAs plays a pivotal role. Corollary, as already highlighted, in conventional terms, arguments in their favour draw on the gains of market integration, where liberalisation leads to gains of *static welfare* and *dynamic* nature. The *static welfare* gains are predicated on increased competition. The extra imports from the EU, induced by *lower prices* (*trade creation*) will be channelled to the ACP consumers in terms of *price advantage*. The *dynamic benefits* for the ACP economies will result from (i) increased levels of investments, (ii) *lock-in effect* of domestic policy reforms[22], (iii) conventional gains from rigorously implemented regional integration, etc.[23]

However, the co-operation between the EU and its ACP associates does in fact present a special case of merging "low performance" and "high performance" regions[24] and therefore has implications that go beyond those assumed under normal

---

[22] The logic behind this is that ACP trade reforms can be sustained if there is enhanced co-operation with the EU, in which case the latter will play the role of an "agency of restraint". In this way, the credibility of the micro-economic and legal framework will be enhanced.

[23] Enhanced investor confidence, due to *inter alia*, (i) assured *market access* (created by a FTA), (ii) dynamic gains characteristic of rigorously implemented regional integration in the aftermath of a REPA, etc.

[24] Many integration schemes involve economies at more or less the same level of economic development. However, even within the *Vinerian integration theory* integration schemes involving developed and developing economies are recognised, a typical case being the LC. Technically the LC presented a form

integration schemes. Though the dimensions of changes may differ, the dynamics of integration schemes that merge developed (high performance) and developing (low performance) economies are the same. However, in addition to the conventional effects, there are some unique gains attributable to the merging of high performance and low performance areas. These include *upward convergence*[25] in various aspects, i.e., systematic upward convergence of levels of income, environmental standards, improved growth, etc. (Cohen 1993, IDIL 1998, Matambalya 1999c, Reynolds 1993, Whiting 1993). Moreover, usually the low performance economies are likely to bear greater costs of integration, at least in the short-run, and, of course, arguments for enhanced lock-in effects remain valid in the long-run.

B. Practical orientation of the EPA model of development co-operation
a. Regional or country focus of development co-operation

In the agreement, ACP regions, sub-regions or countries, will form the loci of EU-ACP co-operation arrangements. The initial proposal within the framework of REPAs envisaged co-operation based on whole regions for the Caribbean and Pacific ACP states, and on sub-regions for the ACP members from Africa (taking into account, among other things, the large number of ACP members). However, the option for individual ACP states to enter a partnership agreement with the EU was left open and was explicitly referred to.[26] In the new agreement, the ACP countries individually or plurally could, according to the provision of *self-selection*, choose the most appropriate basis for their future trade link to the EU.

With regional to regional or country focus, *differentiation* among developing countries as stipulated by the WTO, will be an essential aspect of EPAs, in which context differential treatment will be applied both *between* and *within* regions. As explicitly outlined in the agreement:

"... economic and trade co-operation shall be implemented in full conformity with the provisions of the WTO, including special and differential treatment, taking into account the parties mutual interests and their respective levels of development". [27]

Hence, the co-operation programmes between the EU and the ACP regions, sub-regions, or countries, will be differentiated by such criteria as location, level of economic development, unique needs, past performance, etc.

Intra-regional differentiation is a serious consideration in relation to regional integration, particularly bearing in mind that all regions contain a mixture of LDCs and LLDCs. Apparently, regional EPAs can only be formed among countries at the same level of development. Implicitly, unless a working formula is found, an LDC participating in an EPA which also contains LDCs will have to compromise any

---

of preferential trade area (PTA), involving non-reciprocal trade preferences (Matambalya 1999, Winters 1992).

25 "Upward convergence" means that those starting at the low end systematically move up to-wards those at the high end, in such a way that the ones at the high end do not go down (Reynolds 1993).
26 The recent EU-South Africa Trade, Development and Co-operation Agreement (TDCA) highlights what can be expected of future EU-ACP links within the framework of EPAs
27 Partnership Agreement between the African, Caribbean and Pacific States and the European Community and its Members: Article 34(4).

benefits that might have resulted from "positive differentiation". Hence, the often-emphasised differentiation in favour of LLDCs may be pre-empted by EPAs. Probably because of the implicit complexities that will be involved in its enforcement, there has been no debate as yet about incorporating some kind of *variable geometry* provisions (to grant more favourable treatment to LLDCs) within the framework of EPA involving ACP countries at various levels of development.

b. Scope and approach of liberalisation

A key feature of EPAs is that they will be open to *asymmetrical* liberalisation. This underscores the resolve to make EPAs tailor-made arrangements that match the levels of development of the involved ACP states, in accordance with *article 34(4)*. To concretise:

(a) In terms of market access, the LLDCs among the ACP economies may, depending on the agreement reached after the detailed negotiation, continue to enjoy market access to the EU under the *acquis actuel* (which in essence means that they will retain non-reciprocal trade privileges, and that such an approach will be in line with the special and differential treatment provisions of the WTO). The LDCs among the ACP economies will have to reciprocate EU preferences through the reduction of tariffs on most imports from the EU.

(b) Within the framework of asymmetrical liberalisation, the transition phase will take 10 to 12 years, which is also generally assumed to conform to WTO provisions.

A significant improvement on the initial REPA proposal is that EPAs will cover not only merchandise trade, but also trade in services as well as co-operation in trade related issues. Chapter 4 on trade in services reaffirms, *inter alia*, the resolve to pursue liberalisation in services in accordance with the provisions of the General Agreement on Trade in Services (GATS), and particularly those relating to the participation of developing countries in liberalisation arrangements (*Article 41(4)*) and the need for special and differential treatment to all ACP suppliers of services arrangements (*Article 41(2)*).

Also, liberalisation will have to cover *substantially all trade*. Explicitly this means that there should not be too many products classified as *sensitive* and hence excluded from trade liberalisation.

3.1.2. Essential pillars of the EPA model of development co-operation

A. Integrated approach to development strategies

An interactive co-operation strategy linking the development strategies and the trade and economic partnership agreements, constitutes a key aspect of the agreement. In this respect, the agreement presents a comprehensive and integrated vision of development strategies, which revolve around the prime strategy of poverty reduction.

B. Political dimension

As regards the political dimension, the agreement stresses political dialogue as an integral aspect of the partnership. Such a dialogue should provide a platform under which the parties will, in a more objective and transparent way, discuss fundamental development issues and any subjects of mutual interest. In this context, the essential elements embraced under the umbrella of political dimension include:

(a) Respect for human rights.
(b) Democratic principles.
(c) Rule of law.
(d) Promoting good governance and fighting corruption.

At their February 2000 meeting, the EU and ACP states also discussed at length the various aspects of migration, notably the difficult and, for each of them, extremely sensitive issue of preventing and combating illegal immigration. They came to a balanced agreement enshrining the principle of co-operation on this issue. Accordingly, the EU and the ACP States will initiate a process aimed ultimately at defining - within a framework to be negotiated with each ACP country - the ways and means of repatriating immigrants illegally present on the territories of each party.

This new dimension in EU-ACP co-operation reflects the guidelines espoused by the EU in accordance with the Treaty of Amsterdam and with the conclusions of the European Council held in Tampere (Finland) in October 1999. Corollary, the EU undertakes to develop and implement an immigration and asylum policy founded on the principle of partnership with the originating countries and regions. The Agreement concluded with the ACP countries paves the way for new initiatives, in particular on the rights of third country citizens within the EU and measures facilitating their integration.

Furthermore, the Agreement lends a new democratic dimension to the partnership by actively encouraging the involvement of civil society and non-state actors in the various day-to-day facets of the partnership (political, social, economic and trade), and makes provision for informing and consulting those new actors and strengthening their capacities.

C. Financial resources

Concerning financial co-operation, the 9th European Development Fund (EDF) and European Investment Bank (EIB) resources to be extended to the ACP economies will be worth a total of EURO 15.2 billion. Of this, the EDF resources will amount to EURO 13.5 billion, of which EURO 10 billion will be for the long-term financial envelope, EURO 1.3 billion for the regional envelope and EURO 2.2 billion for the investment facility. The remaining EURO 1.7 billion will be made up of EIB loans.

It has also been agreed that this amount, plus the outstanding balances of previous funds (EURO 10 billion), will cover the period 2000-2007. The Commission has made a political undertaking to ensure, with those resources and over that period, a significant increase in disbursements for the ACP States.

Concretely, the disbursements could be doubled compared with the current situation to reach EURO 3.5 billion per annum.

An innovation of the financial co-operation involves the reforming of the programming of EU aid, by subjecting it to regular reviews based on an analysis of needs and performance of the ACP economies.

4. EU-ACP trade within the framework of the EPA model of development co-operation

The trade chapter builds on the agreement that was achieved in December 1999. Then, the parties agreed on the general approach to trade, particularly on the principles, objectives and schedule for the implementation of the future *economic partnership agreements*. In broad terms, the agreement laid down the foundation for EU-ACP co-operation during the immediate post-Lomé IV transitional phase to EPAs, and the implementation of EPAs.

4.1. Preparatory phase

The LC expired formally in February 2000. Therefore we are at present in the transitional phase to EPAs. During this phase, the Lomé IV equivalent trade arrangements will continue to govern EU-ACP trade relations. The transitional phase, which started running in March 2000, will expire in September 2008.

Procedurally, *article 37* stipulates, among other things, the decision by the EU and ACP states:

(a) To start in September 2002 formal negotiations (to be concluded by 2008 at the latest) on *new WTO-compliant arrangements*. The new WTO-compatible trade regime will phase out the remaining barriers to EU-ACP trade and bolster co-operation in all trade-related fields. Besides, the envisaged trade arrangements will be reciprocal and will take into consideration the *regional integration processes* in the ACP regions and sub-regions.

(b) To evaluate in 2004 the situation of those ACP countries (except for the LLDCs) which have decided that they are unable to negotiate EPAs. The EU will then review the possible alternatives in order to offer the countries involved new trade frameworks equivalent to their existing situation in *compliance with WTO rules*.

(c) To initiate a process in 2000 which, by the end of the multi-lateral trade negotiations and at the latest by 2005, will allow duty-free access for essentially all products from the LLDCs among the ACP states.[28]

(d) To evaluate the impact of the multi-track (i.e., bilateral and multilateral) liberalisation processes, bearing in mind that they erode the preferences

---

[28] The framework agreement declares that the principle of *non-discrimination* among ACP States should not stand in the way of unilateral measures to improve market access to which the EU has committed itself for the LLDCs.

extended to the ACP countries and thereby affecting their competitiveness. The purpose of this evaluation will be to enable the ACP countries and their EU partners to take the necessary remedial measures.

(e) To embark on capacity building in the public and private sector of the ACP countries so as to enhance competitiveness and regional integration.

4.2. Interim phase

The WTO recognises that interim agreements are necessary in order to avoid the economic disturbance likely to be caused by a rapid move to free trade among the member states. Accordingly, following the wishes of the EU states and their ACP partners, the EPAs will be implemented over a transitional period starting at the latest in 2008. After entering into force, the EPAs will, during the interim phase, be progressively manoeuvred towards WTO compatible free trade areas (FTAs). The interim phase will last for 10 to 12 years, and again this is assumed to be in conformity with the WTO requirements (i.e., *article XXIV*). Thus, full WTO compatible FTAs between the EU and its ACP associates will not be in place until 2018 or 2020.

4.3. Summarising remarks

The *Framework Agreement* is, *prima facie*, fairly flexible, leaving all options open. For instance, LDCs which decide that they are not in a position to enter into an EPA with the EU can decide on an optional arrangement which, as the framework agreement assures, will guarantee them market access equivalent to the existing situation (which invariably means, equivalent to the Lomé IV situation).

Despite these promises, it is very obvious that the EU leans heavily in favour of two courses of action:

(a) The establishment of trade regimes modelled upon EPAs.

(b) The assurance of WTO conformity of EPAs or any other optional arrangements.

5. *The EPA model of development co-operation and the WTO*

5.1. WTO compatibility of trade regimes: overview of the general requirements

The WTO is in principle for regional integration and regional trade arrangements. While many articles of the agreement may eventually be relevant for regional trade arrangements, a number of articles are particularly important. For analytical purposes, we will categorise these articles as core articles, or supplementary articles.[29] The pertinent articles are briefly discussed below.

---

[29] For those interested in a more technical analysis of issues discussed in this part and part 5.2, we recommend Matambalya and Wolf "The Cotonou Agreement and the Challenges of Making it WTO Compatible" (forthcoming), Journal of World Trade, Vol. Number 34, February 2001.

5.1.1. Core WTO articles relevant for regional trade regimes

Three articles of the WTO regime present the core provisions on the basis of which a regional trade arrangement can be designed.

(a) *Article XXIV* of the general agreements on trade and tariffs (GATT), revised in 1994. This article guides the formulation of customs territories, i.e., *Free Trade Areas* (FTAs) and *Customs Unions* (CUs). It is meant to ensure that regional trade arrangements facilitate trade between members without raising barriers to trade with third parties (in which case it refers to other GATT contracting parties). Technically, this article presents an exception to *article 1* on the most-favoured nation (MFN) rule.

(b) The *Enabling Clause*, particularly *paragraph 4(a)* and part IV (i.e., Trade and Development of the GATT). This clause, which is a result of the Tokyo Round (1979), provides a legal basis for developed country preferences in favour of developing countries through differential and more favourable treatment. Paragraph 1 of the enabling clause states that:

> " ... notwithstanding the provisions of *article 1* of the General Agreement, contracting parties may accord differential and more favourable treatment to developing countries, without according such treatment to other countries ..."

Therefore, preferential tariff treatment under GSP falls under this clause as well. Furthermore, the enabling clause allows preferences among independent developing countries and is good for South-South regionalisation schemes. Technically, this article also presents an exception to *article 1* on the MFN.

(c) Article V of the GATS.

5.1.2. Supplementary WTO articles relevant for regional trade regimes

Three further articles complement the core articles:

(a) Article 1 on the most favoured nation (MFN) rule. This article prescribes non-discrimination as a central tenet of multilateral trade policy. It is the cornerstone of the WTO trade regime, according to which each WTO member country extends MFN treatment to all other WTO member states.

(b) *Article IX* of the Marrakech Agreement (1994), formerly *Article XXV* of the GATT, on *waivers*. A waiver is granted outside GATT consistent trade arrangements.

(c) *Article XXVIII bis*. Although reciprocity is not explicitly defined in the GATT, this article stipulates that "... *tariff reductions should be on reciprocal and mutually advantageous basis ...*". Exceptions to this article exist through the principles of non-reciprocity and differentiation in the case of developing countries and regional arrangements generally.

5.2. Necessity to make the regime to guide future EU-ACP trade WTO compatible

The reason why a waiver has been necessary for the Lome trade regime is that the regime violated the WTO provisions. Notably:

(a) By providing access to the EU market to only ACP products, it violated the MFN principle of non-discrimination. Furthermore, legal justification did not emerge from article XXIV on FTAs and CUs either, due to one-sided liberalisation, (i.e., the LC did not impose any obligations on ACP economies), and the exclusion of the non-ACP developing economies from similar arrangements.

(b) To the extent that the LC covered services, it violates article V of GATS. This point gains more significance, since (as opposed to the LC, which was mainly concerned with trade in tangible goods) the EPAs are also explicitly intended to cover trade in services.

Thus, the trade regime of the LC has all along been substantially different from a customs territory. Explicitly, since EU-ACP trade during the preparatory phase are modelled upon the LC, they cannot be taken into the interim phase, as they do not conform to the WTO provisions.

Another crucial development in this respect is the unilateral decision by the EU in 1997 to extend LC-equivalent preferences to non-ACP LLDCs. However, it still discriminates the non-ACP LDCs. Therefore, both the LC and the trade regime applicable during the preparatory phase are not WTO compatible and need a waiver through article XXV

Nevertheless, the envisaged introduction of *reciprocity in trade relations* between the EU and its ACP associates necessitates reforms of the trade regime to adapt it to the new realities. Such reforms will, *inter alia*, require the ACP states to introduce a higher degree of reciprocity, so that EU exports on ACP markets will enjoy *improved* MFN status. However, there is also consensus that, at the current level of development of the ACP economies, liberalisation should be *asymmetrical*.[30] In this regard, the push is towards the establishment of FTAs within the framework of EPAs.

5.3. Options to make EPAs WTO compatible: initial reflections

Both conceptual and practical dimensions are necessary to attain WTO compatibility of any trade regime. Technically, the envisaged trade regime under

---

[30] In this context, the EU is making two proposals with respect to liberalisation:
- Asymmetry with respect to the *time requirements for the implementation of the liberalisation plan*, in which case the EU will liberalise faster than the ACP economies.
- Asymmetry regarding the *scope of trade to be liberalised*, where the EU will liberalise more comprehensively (i.e., a higher percentage of total trade) than the ACP economies.

EPAs falls within a North-South regionalisation arrangement. Therefore, the foregoing discussion suggests that at the conceptual level, inasmuch as reciprocity is involved, both the ACP states and EU states will be obliged only to discriminate within the provisions of the exceptions to article 1 of the GATT.

In practical terms, the viable options include, (i) opting for a WTO consistent convention, (ii) opting for a WTO inconsistent convention and bargaining for waivers.

5.3.1. Opting for a WTO consistent convention

Analogous to the arguments above, a WTO compatible FTA can be designed on the basis of *Article XXIV* of the general agreements on trade and tariffs (GATT) and/or the *Enabling Clause*, which allows developed country preferences in favour of developing countries.

A. WTO consistent within the framework of Article XXIV

Empirical observations suggest that article XXV is most suited for North-North trade arrangements because of its requirements for comprehensive liberalisation that usually go beyond the will of most developing economies. Nevertheless, the article makes provision for asymmetrical liberalisation, which makes it suitable for North-South trade regimes as well.

Notably, Article XXIV facilitates four types of regional arrangements:

(a) An interim arrangement leading to an FTA.
(b) An FTA.
(c) An interim arrangement leading to a customs union (CU).
(d) A CU.

Furthermore, although it is stipulated that after the interim period the trade regime should cease to be asymmetrical, reciprocity must not be granted in full. What is important is that it shall cover substantially all trade.

B. Consistency within the framework of the Enabling Clause

In contrast to Article XXV the Enabling Clause was deliberately conceived with the interests of developing countries in mind. Hence, its primary objective is to facilitate development, while trade plays a secondary role.

5.3.2. Opting for a WTO inconsistent convention and bargaining for a waiver

Any EPA that does not satisfy the conditions set in articles, when jointly interpreted, is likely to be WTO inconsistent, and can only be pushed through by a waiver permitting derogation from MFN. According to past practices, the legal obligation to apply for a waiver lies with the EU. Procedurally, this is a co-ordinated administrative process involving both the EU and the ACP as follows:

(a) The Commission of the EU prepares a draft, which is then distributed to the ACP for comment, or for noting (if the ACP states do not desire to make any comments).

(b) Any ACP comments are incorporated and the necessary modifications made.

(c) The text is then forwarded to the WTO with a covering letter signed by the EU and endorsed by the Chair of the ACP Committee of Ambassadors.

(d) The ACP and EU jointly defend the application.

The disadvantage of a waiver is that it does not provide a sustainable solution and, to go through, it must be supported by at least 75 percent of WTO members. The combined strength of the ACP WTO members (55) and EU (15) is 70, which out of the total WTO membership of 135 is equivalent to 52 percent.[31] Therefore, at the current standing, support from an additional 31 members is necessary to attain at least 75 percent of vote.

Furthermore, even if granted, a waiver does not offer waterproof protection of the preferential arrangements. Concretely, despite the granting of a waiver, special preferences to the ACP states can be challenged by any other WTO member. Indeed, a waiver request dated 2.03.2000 has already been submitted to the relevant authorities at the WTO Secretariat. So far, it has succumbed to the banana litigation (cf. Matambalya and Wolf, forthcoming, *Journal Of World Trade*, Vol. 34, No. 1).

5.3.3. Other viable and less contentious considerations

Apart from the fundamental legal requirements of compliance with the WTO, the EU and their ACP partners may consider several options for modelling the trade regime of their development co-operation. In this regard, the three basic options, which could form the basis for further deliberations are:

(i) *Modelling the EPA trade regime upon multi-lateral liberalisation* in line with WTO provisions.

(ii) *Opening up the partnership for all developing economies* and seeking reform of the WTO to address the special requirements of developing countries. This globalisation of EU-ACP co-operation makes sense to the degree that the goal of future development co-operation is to expedite global development as opposed to pursue special group interests. In this case, it makes sense to treat countries at the same level of development equally (Matambalya 1999: 243).

(iii) Within the framework of the EPA model for development co-operation, *separating co-operation in trade from co-operation in other aspects*. Thereafter, the EU-ACP trade regime can be modelled on multilateral arrangements within the framework of the WTO-compliant provisions as in (i), and even extended to all developing countries as in (ii).

In addition, it is possible to think of more basic options, as well as hybrid options which can be derived from the basic options.

---

[31] The Kingdom of Jordan accessed the WTO in April 2000, bringing the number of its members to 136.

5.3.4. Summarising remarks

Although the analysis in this part (i.e., on options on how to make EPAs WTO compatible) is merely informed speculation over issues still *sub judice*, where the final outcome may be politically flavoured, it is likely that nothing short of significant reforms will salvage the traditional trade links between the EU and their ACP associates. In part 5.4 we briefly highlight, among other things, the possible areas of reform.

5.4. Adequacy of WTO provisions to provide the legal base for a future EU-ACP trade regime and possible areas for reform

In principle article XXIV and the Enabling Clause, in conjunction with other WTO provisions, provide a legal base for all forms of postulated trade regimes. However, a close look at the pertinent provisions reveals that they all contain inherent deficiencies that may need to be reformed in order to facilitate the establishment of an advanced form of North-South integration, as envisaged by the EPA model of development co-operation. In concrete terms, the caveats related to both Article XXIV and the Enabling Clause are articulated by the ambiguity of these provisions when it comes to details.

5.4.1. Caveats related to Article XXIV

A conspicuous deficiency of Article XXIV is that it does not specify what a WTO compatible FTA should cover, beyond the stipulation that they should *cover substantially all trade*. Explicitly this means that there should not be too many products classified as "sensitive" and hence excluded from trade liberalisation. The WTO provisions remain silent in terms of concrete indicators or thresholds, and what "substantially all trade" means remains contentious. This situation has led to different interpretations. Going by recent EU interpretations, a WTO compatible FTA should: (i) cover around 90 percent of total trade, (ii) not exclude any sector from the trade liberalisation agreement, (iii) have a duration of 10 to 12 years.

A further deficiency is the lack of precision in the interpretation of "constituent customs territories". It is not clear whether they refer to only economically contagious customs territories (i.e., involving countries at the same level of development), or it refers also to geographically contagious customs territories (i.e., involving regions forming a continuous land mass) (*paragraph 4*). Even if it is assumed that the provision refers to both (Thomas 1997), this leads to another problem, namely that the provision did not consider the prospect of geographically non-contagious customs territories as would be implied by an integration involving the EU and the EC economies. Also, the inadequacy of the article to address many key issues related to integration suggests that it was not conceived to facilitate a higher degree of merging developed and developing economies.

It is noteworthy that so far only the EU has been ruled to be GATT/WTO compatible under Article XXIV

5.4.2. Caveats related to the Enabling Clause

Concerning this clause, while *Article XXIV(5)* stipulates that *".. members' duties and regulations of commerce should not be higher or more restrictive than the corresponding ones existing prior to the formation of an FTA ..."*, it is not clear whether the duties referred to are *bound rates* or *applied rates*.

Also, though the Clause provides the basis for *special and differential treatment* (SDT)[32], so far there is no experience with differentiation between LDCs and LLDCs. On the whole, the enabling clause is criticised for being less tangible and for its nebulous definitions (Thomas 1997).

On the whole, these ambiguities surrounding the various WTO provisions magnify the problem of reaching consensus and also lead to abuse.

5.4.3. Caveats related to the Waiver

The waiver is inherently deficient and has all along been classified as not being WTO-consistent. Besides, under the GATT rules of 1994, it is only granted on an annual basis and requires approval by 75 percent of the WTO Council membership. Also, it does not offer watertight protection, and can be disputed by any WTO member. The banana litigation exposes the limitations of a waiver in contemporary international trade relations (cf. Matambalya and Wolf, forthcoming, *Journal of World Trade*, Vol. 34, No. 1).

6. *Potential precipitators and hindrances to the implementation of EPAs*
6.1. Technical impediments

Besides the political will, strongly underscored through the conclusion of the negotiations for the *Framework Agreement*, and in addition to the requirements for WTO compatibility, certain conditions must be fulfilled if EPAs are to be smoothly implemented. In the immediate to medium term, these conditions are manifested by a multitude of technical factors, including:

(a) The *underdeveloped status of integration* in regions and sub-regions. This is important, if ACP regions and/or sub-regions are to be EU partners in EPAs.

(b) The *absence or underdevelopment of supranational institutions of integration* in the various ACP regions. Notably, since in the long-run FTAs will be the hub of the EPAs, it will be necessary to establish and/or consolidate supranational institutions in the ACP regions and sub-regions and to create similar capacity at national levels in order to manage the separate sub-regional or national level

---

[32] This implies the need to accord further special treatment to developing countries, as covered by Enabling Clause of the WTO.

EPAs.

(c) The implications of *merging low and high-income regions* on the one hand, and geographically significantly separated regions on the other. So far, inadequate studies of the impact of such mergers have been done. Hence, there is no reliable information basis for planning action.

(d) The resolve to promote seemingly conflicting goals, like *regional integration* and *differential treatment* particularly between LLDCs and LDCs from the same regions, without making clear suggestions on how to achieve this, etc.

(e) The complicated geography of regionalisation. The matters are further complicated by the fact that the ACP group of nations are experiencing a resurgence and proliferation of regionalisation schemes, many of which overlap in terms of country membership.

(f) The restricted competency of the ACP to negotiate. The limited resources and the urgency of the matter puts the ACP states at a disadvantage straight away. Judging from past experience, it is hard to imagine most of the individual ACP economies being able to build capacity in time to make detailed professional analyses of the available opportunities and their implications, and thereby make rational decisions and useful contributions to the ACP position.

6.2. Framework for institutional linkages and modalities for preferential treatment

An FTA is the minimum requirement for a trade regime that conforms to the WTO regulations. Hence, reforms will be necessary in at least three major areas which are significant for the co-operation between the two partner groupings: trade regime, institutional linkages and the modalities for preferential treatment.

There is a potential conflict between EPAs and multi-lateral liberalisation obligations of the EU and ACP economies. While most (currently 55) ACP economies subscribe to the WTO, the implementation of EPAs will overlap with multi-lateral reforms within the framework of WTO. Hence, technically there might be pressure for the ACP states to generalise the *improved* market access they extend to the EU and to other trade partners as well. In the event of a "global extension" of liberalisation, the scale of the competitive and fiscal impact of EPAs will be influenced, and the costs of liberalisation may be compounded.

7. *Summary of merits and demerits of the EPA model of development co-operation*

At this stage some observations can be made regarding the strengths and shortfalls of EPAs. The potential merits of the EPA model include:

(a) An obvious improvement on the REPA proposal is that the *Framework Agreement* has extended its scope and provisions, and thus in the EPA proposal, it presents a comprehensive development co-operation model addressing diverse issues of significance to the development of the ACP states.

(b) Because of the refocusing of the loci for development co-operation, EPAs will respond more adequately to the specific requirements of the individual ACP economies/regions. They will respond more directly to the needs and priorities set by the ACP economies/regions.

(c) To the extent that they will enhance regional integration in the various ACP regions/sub-regions, EPAs will reduce the prospects for trade deflection away from ACP regions to the EU.

(d) EPAs will enhance the integration of the ACP economies into the world economy.

(e) Higher prospects for upward convergence can be associated with EPAs.

(f) EPAs are also likely to enhance the lock-in effects. This will be manifested through, among other things, the stabilisation of policies (e.g., in trade and investment), thus enhancing the confidence of potential investors.

(g) EPAs are likely to offer a stable basis for development co-operation. This is because of their WTO compatibility, which means that in future there will be no need for recourse to special requirements like waivers and the uncertainties associated with the process.

Despite the obvious merits of EPAs discussed in the preceding paragraph, this new model of development co-operation is still deficient in many ways. This is partly because some of the demerits of the Lomé Convention and the original REPA proposal have been carried forward into the EPA model. These limitations, which have varying influence on not only the EPA as a trade regime, but also the EPA as a development co-operation model as a whole, are manifested by:

(a) The poor articulation of the *real and potential impediments* in establishing EPAs between the EU and virtually all the ACP regions and sub-regions.

(b) The failure to explicitly and directly address the real impediments to the development of the ACP economies, which centre around the restricted productivity of these economies.

(c) The often cited flexibility of EPAs is indeed a *manifestation of flexibility in a cage*. To the extent that the operational framework is already laid down by the WTO, the emphasised flexibility is deceitful.

(d) Considering what is necessary to generate sustainable economic development, it is obvious that the resources committed to EDF 9 remain far below the critical mass. Even if we double the resources and divide them with the (current) population (hence assuming stagnation of the ACP population), the annual disbursements per head to ACP citizens will only be around 10 Euros.

(e) Inherent ambiguity. This arises from the fact that EPAs foresee differential treatment of LLDCs and LDCs among the ACP states. Hence, LLDCs may be discouraged from participating in integration schemes, thereby complicating the geography of regionalisation and weakening the regionalisation schemes altogether. Also, measures such as the recent EU-South African Agreement, which in effect de-links South Africa from its Southern African neighbours, cast a shadow of doubt on the logic of development co-operation as a whole.

III KEY ISSUES TO BE ADDRESSED BY THE EASTERN AND SOUTHERN AFRICAN STATES IN THE WAKE OF POST-LOMÉ IV EU-ACP CO-OPERATION

8. Necessary conditions for functional EPAs between the EU and the ACP states

From the foregoing discussion, it is obvious that while the EPA model of development co-operation will further pursue the overall purpose of promoting development in the ACP states, it is also clear that its trade regime will only be able to extend to the ACP states trade incentives within the framework of multilateralism. Hence, three important issues arise as necessary conditions to be fulfilled, if the envisaged EPAs are to become functional and effective. These are: the clarity of their development co-operation agenda; their adherence to international obligations; and their institutional capacities.

8.1. Clarity of development co-operation agenda

The regionalisation of EU-ACP co-operation will call for a clear articulation of the development co-operation agenda of the various regions and sub-regions. Such agendas should decompose the development requirements into aspects that can at best be dealt with at the national, regional and global levels respectively.

The prospects of a significant share of funds being re-allocated from the National Indicative Programme (NIP) makes this consideration necessary, while past experience with regional projects suggests tough going. Notably, to the extent that regional projects express the clarity of regional development agendas, past experiences are not very encouraging. The articulation of regional projects has been one of the major problems of regional groupings, as exemplified by the SADC. A review of the SADC programme of action (SPA) conducted between 1996 and 1997 revealed that only 22 percent (in number) and 12 percent (in value terms) of all projects declared by the member states as regional, really qualified to be classified as such (Matambalya 1999d).

8.2. Adherence to international obligations of the ACP and EU states

In this regard, the most pressing demand will be compliance with the provisions of the WTO. Hence formulating a new trade regime will involve the delicate task of reconciling seemingly extremely diverging objectives and coming up with a convention that is broadly acceptable not only to all parties bound by the contract, but also to other actors in the international system. Concretely, this will mean balancing:

(a) WTO compatibility and ACP demands for preferential access (in view of the fact that there is as yet *no level playing field* to justify the all embracing and significant ACP-EU reciprocity), besides the desire to maintain the *historical* links with the EU.

(b) EU's interests (which are underscored by not only its mercantilist motives, but also by its interest to uphold the long-standing relations with its ACP associates).[33]

---

[33] The *mercantilist motive* stresses the market access considerations of the EU. Proponents of this argument (whom McQueen refers to as the *mercantilist lobby* in the Union), see in the Free Trade

8.3. Institutional requirements

The inadequacies of supranational institutions are among the biggest challenges in establishing EPAs between the EU and its ACP associates. Nevertheless, a regionally focused multi-tier arrangement will pose special institutional requirements in order to effectively manage the co-operation. In reality, both regional supra-national institutions (to facilitate the efficient management of regionally-focused co-operation) and transregional (in the likely event that the ACP group remains intact) supra-national bodies (to uphold ACP solidarity) will be needed. Hence, the enhancement of supra-national institutions at the regional and sub-regional levels is imperative.[34] In this regard, it is expedient to enhance the institutional efficiency of the sub-regions in order to facilitate communication between the secretariat and these regions, as well as among the sub-regions.

Also at the global level, the scope of impending changes makes the restructuring of the ACP secretariat indispensable. Hence, though it is still convenient to maintain a joint secretariat, this secretariat needs radical reforms to enable it to more adequately address the requirements of the various regions and sub-regions, and to more competently interact with the EU.

For the new system to work, a decentralisation of the ACP activities is inevitable. As suggested in Appendix I, it will be advantageous to establish a few General Directorates (GDs), along-side Regional Directorates (RDs). In addition, the ACP regions and sub-regions which have the requisite resources should contemplate establishing autonomous regional offices in Brussels. While the Caribbean Regional Negotiating Machinery (Caribbean RNM) in London could serve as a model, it may be necessary to improve upon this model (in both qualitative and quantitative terms) to come up with fully functional regional representation offices.[35]

9. Challenges and nebulous issues

Several key issues in the regionalisation of the linkages between Eastern and Southern Africa and the EU will also need to be carefully assessed. The most

---

Arrangement (FTA) associated with REPAs the means for capturing markets, while at the same time domestically protecting industries and sensitive sectors, suggesting that the EU sees in the FTAs associated with REPAs a means for capturing markets, while at the same time domestically protecting industries and sensitive sectors. Finally, it should also be reiterated that there still exist sufficient pressure groups within the EU, particularly within the Non-Governmental Organisation (NGO) sector, which recognise the essence for the continuation of the historically long-standing and strong EU-ACP linkages (Matambalya 1999b: 262, McQueen 1998: 673).

[34] The SADC, for example, inherited from SADCC a deliberate policy of sectoral co-ordination by member countries, designed to minimise the burden of supra-national institutions. As such, the secretariat in Gaborone is not equipped to handle a big volume of assignments (Matambalya 1999b, Matambalya 1995).Therefore, it is infeasible to think of the same institutions enforcing both intra-regional integration, and a REPA with the EU.

[35] Theoretically, the ACP regions and sub-regions can choose between having separate and independent representations in Brussels, maintaining a joint ACP secretariat, or having a mixture of both regional and global institutions.

prominent among them include: the proliferation of regionalisation schemes in the region which is further associated with multiple memberships; the status of COMESA; the implications of the process to de-link South Africa from the region; the dysfunctionality of institutions; the risk of chronically dysfunctional state; and the overall state of underdevelopment of integration in the region.

9.1 Proliferation of integration schemes

The proliferation of regionalisation schemes is one of the greatest challenges to the determination of the appropriate "geography of regionalisation" in Eastern and Southern Africa. Currently, the region hosts 4 major integration schemes (i.e., COMESA, EAC, SACU and SADC), with one integration programme (i.e., the IOC) systematically consolidating itself. Besides, there are 3 more integration schemes: (i) the Common Monetary Area (CMA); (ii) Intergovernmental Authority on Development (IGAD); and (iii) the Indian Ocean Rim Association for Regional Co-operation (IORARC). Moreover, several countries in the region maintain bilateral arrangements in different forms, e.g., development corridors. Such arrangements exist between, for example, Mozambique and Tanzania, Tanzania and Zambia. Besides, some countries of the region are involved in "cross-border initiatives" (CBIs).

Overall, these developments cast a shadow of doubt over the economic and political relevance of the regionalisation schemes. It also does the same for the economic and political identity of the region, even when it is separated into East Africa and Southern Africa. Besides economic and political motives, there is a strong indication that the growing number of integration schemes may be sparked by opportunistic motives. Increasingly, regionalisation schemes seem to resemble "clubs" through which member countries or interest groups pursue their vested interests, in particular to attract funds from donor institutions. This leads to a "thin-spreading of resources", leading to wastage and sub-optimal results.

9.2. Status of COMESA

The COMESA represents a special case related to integration schemes in the region. Generally, it is hard to imagine (in the short-term) an EPA based on the regional coverage of the COMESA. The obvious limitations include the great disparities in such basic dimensions as the cultural, religious and ethnic backgrounds of the people in the region. The disparities in economic and political development pose further challenges. Thus, such over-extended regionalisation schemes may cause more harm than good, and even bring the whole integration process to a halt.

However, the arrangement presents a very ambitious trade regime. Pan-Africanism is one of its greatest appeals. Yet, it is not clear what will happen to it, if the economies of Eastern and Southern Africa opt for a regionalisation scheme that does not have the same country composition as COMESA.

Deliberations in this direction, too, may be useful and certainly the future regionalisation schemes in Africa may have something to learn from COMESA.

One solution, for instance, may involve the adoption by the extended regionalisation schemes for Eastern and Southern Africa of the COMESA trade protocol. On its basis, agreements may be extended to current COMESA members which lie too far afield to be logically incorporated in the region's integration schemes.

9.3. Prospect of de-linking South Africa from the region

Besides being a member of the SADC and the SACU, South Africa has signed a separate FTA with the EU. This move poses several challenges and is a source of nebulous issues. *Ipso facto*, it:

(a) complicates South Africa's linkage to the other economies in the region.

(b) denotes incoherent multiple linkages between the region and the EU.

(c) complicates the prospect of adopting integration based on the "degree of regional homogeneity", even if the "pan-Africanist" approach is adopted.

(d) suggests a complex formula of variable geometry, if the region is to remain together as a single partner of the EU, etc.

Thus, South Africa's dilemma will persist, regardless of whether Eastern and Southern Africa is taken as one region, or broken up into sub-regions (e.g., conforming to EAC, IOC and SACU).

9.4. Risk of chronically dysfunctional institutions including the states
9.4.1. General remarks on the dysfunctionality of institutions

One of the key barriers to the enforcement of development programmes in the ACP and other developing countries has been the plight of *dysfunctional institutions*[36] in many of them. At the level of the state, according to the *Green Paper* (EU 1996), for instance, about 11 percent of the population in Africa South of the Sahara was affected by civil war or armed conflicts. Another 30 percent lived in countries that "only just" satisfy minimum criteria for peace and proper economic management (Matambalya 1999e, EU 1996).

The repeated eruption of conflicts, as in recent years manifested by new conflicts in the Democratic Republic of Congo (DRC), Ethiopia, Eritrea, etc., there have been shifts in these percentages. Also, such developments, as the armed conflict in Guinea Bissau, suggest that the problem is still relevant.

Dysfunctional states manipulate the dysfunctionality of institutions at the highest level. Invariably, states suffering from the dysfunctionality of institutions are marred by political instability, resulting in weak government institutions. Weak government institutions, in turn, are attributed to a multitude of tribulations, such as, constrained implementation of government policies, rising crime, falling

---

[36] In its reference to dysfunctional institutions, the *Green Paper* defines countries as *dysfunctional* if they are characterised by political instability, weak government institutions, rising crime, organised violence and armed conflict.

confidence in state institutions by its citizens, etc. In more extreme cases, these deficits permeate the emergence and consolidation of organised violence and armed conflicts.

Consequently, a dysfunctional state is a potential source of problems, with far-reaching implications. Among other things:

(a) It tends to cause much internal havoc. For example civil war and persecution can result in the misplacement of people and gross violation of human rights in general. It also reduces social trust and trust in state institutions.

(b) It has a *ripple effect* on neighbouring countries. Thus a dysfunctional state causes economic and social costs to the neighbouring countries as well, for example as a result of the influx of refugees and migrants. The export of *ideologies of mono-ethnic thinking* is an even more serious threat to regional stability. Sometimes, in order to shun the risk of being engulfed in the conflict, neighbouring states build up arms and maintain economically inviable (large) armies. This fuels investor scepticism and discourages foreign direct investment. The ongoing crisis in the DRC is evidence of this syndrome.

(c) It reduces international confidence in the region. The picture of a war-torn region lingers on long after the end of the actual conflict, giving fuel to investor scepticism and thereby discouraging foreign direct investments (FDI), and encouraging capital flight (Bheenick 1998, Matambalya 1999e).

That an integration process can only be fostered by stable and well-functioning states is well demonstrated by the EU. From the evolution of the EU, we know that although it was partly propelled by the bad experience of the two world wars, *integration did not precede political stability.* Consequently, countries like Greece, Spain and Portugal only qualified to join the integration process after they had successfully eliminated domestic political instability and effectively departed from the culture of military regimes. In fact, to date, political stability is a prime criterion for acceptance as a member state of the EU.

Empirical studies have rated political instability very high among the major causes of the limited achievement of integration in Eastern and Southern Africa (Langhammer and Hiemenz 1990, Matambalya 1995).

9.4.2. Significance for Eastern and Southern Africa

Eastern and Southern Africa as envisaged here, contains the Great Lakes Region (GLR), which in Burundi and Rwanda, hosts two of the chronically most dysfunctional states in Africa, in which even in the current time of great political reforms in Africa, the political mandate still depends on the barrel of the gun rather than the ballot. Recent developments in the DRC, Ethiopia and Eritrea have not helped to ease the situation. Likewise, the prospect of the eruption of large scale military conflict in Uganda, though limited, is still a genuine matter for concern, bearing in mind that several rebel groups are active in the country, which has shunned movement towards multi-party democracy in favour of a *de facto* one party system re-named the "movement".[37]

Also, several states in Eastern and Southern Africa (Angola, Burundi, Eritrea, Ethiopia, Namibia, Rwanda, South Africa, Tanzania, Uganda, and Zimbabwe) have, at one time or another, been "engaged" in the DRC in one way or another. In a sombre expression of *Realpolitik*, Burundi, Rwanda and Uganda still have huge occupation forces in the mineral- and agriculturally-rich Eastern part of the country (in the name of support for the rebel forces), while Angola, Namibia and Zimbabwe officially support the government forces of the DRC. South Africa, the regional superpower, has been accused for selling weapons to both camps involved in the struggle for power in the country.

Altogether, these facts put a big question mark on such states as Burundi and Rwanda in the first place. Despite the international sympathy for the current regimes in both countries, mainly due to the carnage of 1994, both countries remain, *explicit* military regimes with no mandate from the people, and *mono-ethnic* considerations still dictate the political reality and the inter-personal relationships. Thus, they still have a long-way to go, to install viable democratic and *hetero-ethnic* structures. The situation in the Horn of Africa (i.e., the vague peace between Ethiopia and Eritrea and the chronic instability in Somalia) also presents a genuine cause for concern. Generally, with a few exceptions (notably, the IOC states, Kenya, South Africa and Tanzania), stability in most states in the region is elusive.

Therefore, it is hard to see effective integration in a politically unstable region, full of contradictions. The reasons are simple and straight forward: integration with unstable regions will internalise the *ripple effects* of conflicts, inevitably breaking the dynamism of integration, which may eventually lead to the disintegration of integration efforts altogether.

9.4.3. Deficiency in institutions of national unity

The dysfunctionality of states observed in the great Lakes region in Africa may present an extreme, but not exceptional case, if we objectively consider the realities on the ground in Africa. We feel that this situation can be linked to the fact that *institutions of national unity* are, by and large, lacking. In this respect, we use the term *institutions of national unity*, to refer to institutions particularly, but not only, in the public sector, which are unbiased against any individual or social group on the basis of ethno-racial considerations, or on considerations tied to region of origin of the individual or social group concerned.

It is obvious that many African states will not pass a litmus test on the promotion of institutions of social unity. Even in countries which are at rather advanced stages in terms of nation-building and national unity (e.g., the Tanzania of today which by African standards is rightfully hailed for its national unity), it is common to find people in leadership positions who are *mono-ethnic-* or *religiously-biased* in the

---

[37] This provokes uncomfortable memories of the role played by the instability of the country in the demise of the EAC.

way they view and do things. Such leaders are keen to translate the institutions they lead into *predominantly mono-ethnic* or *religiously-cleansed* constructions. Eventually, such institutions serve more as tools of social segregation and national disunity than otherwise. This tendency, which is conspicuous in the public sector, is much worse in conflict-ridden states (e.g., Burundi, DRC, Rwanda, Somalia, etc.), and underpins the need to intensify efforts to promote institutions of national unity.

The phenomenon of faulty institutions of national unity underscores deficiencies belying not only the public, but also the private sector in many African states. As pointed out by Collier and Gunning (1998), economic growth in many African states is constrained by the fact that even the private sector is fractionalised along ethno-racial lines. Also, the author in a survey of small and medium scale enterprises (SMEs) of the SADC economies conducted for the World Intellectual Property Organisation (WIPO) revealed further evidence of faulty institutions in the private sector.

Hence, these developments underscore the need to invest in the creation of minimum adequate conditions for development in quite a number of the countries, before they can be useful members of an effective integration scheme (Collier et al. 1998, Matambalya 1999e). Invariably, the EU and its ACP partners face a gargantuan challenge to design new strategies for the alleviation of conflicts that usually lead to the dysfunctionality of institutions. It seems that conflict prevention and resolution strategies should be part and parcel of the future agenda for development co-operation.

9.5. Underdeveloped status of integration in the region

Analogous to the scenario in other ACP regions, the current level of integration in Eastern and Southern Africa is still below the required threshold to support a functional regionalisation, let alone an ambitious development co-operation scheme à la EPA. For instance, although the SADC trade protocol was signed in 1996, to date it has not yet been ratified by all member states. Also intra-regional trade remains low, almost two decades since the inception of integration efforts in Southern Africa through the Southern African Development Co-ordination Conference (SADCC). When South Africa is excluded, intra-SADC trade is only about 5 percent (IDIL 1999, Matambalya 1999b, Matambalya 1995).

The picture for East Africa is not much better. Although the EAC brings together countries with a long common history, language and strong affinities in other cultural aspects, economic integration remains low. In 1995, Kenya's imports from and exports to the other two EAC members were only 1.1 percent and 9.3 percent respectively. The figures for Tanzania were 4.5 percent and 5.4 percent respectively, while those for Uganda were 2.2 percent and 3.9 percent respectively. (CREDIT 1998). In addition, the ratification of the treaty establishing the East African Community was substantially delayed.

IV RECOMMENDATIONS AND CONCLUDING REMARKS

10. Reconciling the EPA model of development co-operation and the development requirements of Eastern and Southern Africa

From economic theory we know that in real life situations we very often have to settle for *second best* solutions because *optimal conditions* are hard to secure. Developing a model of development co-operation between the EU and its ACP associates is a typical case for second best solution as it touches on issues of crucial interest to a diverse spectrum of stakeholders. This necessitates concessions from the negotiating parties which block the path to optimality. Bearing this in mind, in the following sections we will reflect on the necessary conditions for making EPAs the second best option of development co-operation between the EU and its ACP associates.

Generally the development efforts of the ACP economies explicitly and implicitly target (i) the development of competitive economies, (ii) further co-operation within the ACP group, (iii) the continued linkages with the EU, (iv) the fostering of regional integration (including the creation of the AEC for the African ACP economies, and (v) the smooth integration in the world economy. They also recognise what is essential in order to attract inward investments, and in order (in the long-run) to diversify their international trade and overall economic relations.

In principle, the regionalisation of EU-ACP co-operation à la EPA presents an innovative and plausible model of development co-operation, and a carefully designed EPA will answer the development requirements of the Eastern and Southern African economies. In this context, the essence of a development co-operation model founded upon differential treatment is underscored by such factors as, (i) the geographical differences and proximities of the various ACP countries, (ii) the diverging development priorities and potentials of the ACP regional groupings, (iii) the relative homogeneity of groups of countries within the ACP that can be joined into economically more plausible groups, (iv) the varying levels of economic development of the various ACP economies, etc. (Matambalya 1999b, 1998, 1997).

If EPAs are to bear the expected fruits in terms of fostering sustainable and self-propelled development, they should be designed in accordance with the realities of contemporary and future development needs of ACP economies. In consequence they should be predicated upon two major classes of considerations, which we refer to as:

(a) *Basic considerations* (related to the geography of regionalisation, the modality of ties, the scope of development co-operation and the functionality of such ties).
(b) *Strategic considerations* (related to trade and overall economic competitiveness).

10.1. Basic considerations

To devise functional, regionally differentiated EU-ACP co-operation arrangements, several basic issues must be considered. These include specifying the "geography of regionalisation"; determining the modality of ties; setting the scope of development co-operation; and creating a base for the functionality of envisaged ties.

10.1.1. "Geography of regionalisation"

One important lesson from the history of economic integration is that it cannot be driven from outside. Analogously, when contemplating the formation of viable ACP regional groupings, it should be borne in mind that the "geography of regionalisation" cannot be driven from outside. Thus, the ACP countries should have a choice in the "geography of regionalisation"

Ideally, the ACP groupings should be as natural as possible, and bear political and practical feasibility. In this regard, they may follow the existing integration schemes, or be built along any other criteria deemed viable by the ACP states themselves. While the Caribbean and Pacific cases are relatively clear due to, among other things, the small numbers of states involved, in Africa the situation is complicated by the proliferation of integration schemes and the overlapping memberships.

In an ideal scenario, the integration schemes in Africa should be based on geographically, politically and economically clearly linked countries. However, reality shows that by and large this does not exist. Even such old integration schemes as the SACU reveal weaknesses because of limited economic and political linkages and skewed interdependencies. Overall, the infancy of integration in Africa means that in reality the window for optional approaches to the "geography of regionalisation" is wide open.

One strategy to counter the dilemma of the proliferation of integration schemes in Africa is to adopt a *pan-Africanist* approach, and form broadly based (supra) integration schemes that could accommodate "smaller" ones within them. Variable geometry can guarantee the continued co-operation within the smaller schemes. To underscore the viability of this option, we learn from the evolution of the EU that the traditional close linkages among the BENELUX states (i.e., Belgium, Netherlands, and Luxembourg) never contradicted their smooth integration in the EU.

10.1.2. Modality of ties: multi-tierism

A. *Multi-tierism and the EPA concept*

Generally, the regionalised EU-ACP linkages can be based on one of three strategic frameworks of ties: a single level and single-tier arrangement; a multi-level and multi-tier arrangement; and separate uncoordinated arrangements.[38] Various

---

[38] In this context a *multi-level and multi-tier arrangement* denotes differentiated co-operation arrangements between the EU and groups of ACP states within the framework of a 'global' co-operation arrangement between the EU and all ACP states. In the second option, the linkages may take the form of *multi-level and multi-tier arrangements* based on a global arrangement to link the EU to all ACP states, and differentiated (regionalised) arrangements to link the EU to specific ACP regions and sub-regions.

combinations of these basic forms to obtain complex arrangements are also possible.[39]

According to the EPA concept, the EU's partners would be whichever countries or groups of countries which wish to enter such an agreement. However, taking all forces into account, a *multi-level and multi-tier co-operation* arrangement presents the most appealing course of action. For the ACP regions and sub-regions it will mean a *global agreement* containing general undertakings and guaranteeing the maintenance of the unity of the ACP group of nations and the EU-ACP supranational links. The *Framework Agreement* is suited to serve this purpose.

The global arrangement will be complemented by a range of *regional agreements* in order to enhance the efficiency of the development co-operation efforts. Desirable country specific programmes could still be contained in the National Indicative Programmes (NIPs), as was the case under the LC. The *EPA Agreements* will serve this purpose.

This approach will preserve the historic links between both the EU and its ACP associates and among the ACP States, as well as enhance the economic efficiency of the links in future.

B. Multi-tierism and ACP's institutional requirements

An important consideration in this regard concerns the role of the *regions* or *sub-regions* in the enforcement of the development co-operation. In this regard, a viable alternative should embrace both institutional rationalisation and the effective representation of regional interests. In the short to medium term it will be necessary to restructure the ACP Secretariat and create *sub-regional departments* to co-ordinate sub-regional matters instead of having several sub-regional offices of the ACP. The latter alternative (having several sub-regional offices of the ACP) may amplify the consultation, co-operation and co-ordination problems which were discernible in all the Lomé Conventions. Also, it will most likely weaken the ACP as a group, and may eventually lead to its disintegration.

The concrete suggestions on how the ACP secretariat can be reformed to meet future requirements are presented in appendix II.

10.1.3. Functionality of ties: consolidation of regional integration

In order to function, EPAs need functional integration schemes in the ACP regions and sub-regions. This is because the ACP economies will have to engage in

---

Finally, there may be a series of *separate and uncoordinated arrangements* between the EU and specified ACP states or groups of states where the ACP groups can be defined along continental lines or otherwise. In other words, the ACP regions would lose their character as a single group and be individually linked to the EU through a *single-level* (and for the EU) *multi-tier arrangement* (Matambalya 1999b, Matambalya 1998, Matambalya 1997).

[39] The *Green Paper*, for instance, offered three options: (i) a global agreement supplemented by bilateral agreements with individual countries or groups of countries (for Sub-Saharan Africa); (ii) regional agreements; and (iii) separate agreements with LLDCs (European Commission 1996: viii-ix and 43-45, Matambalya 1999, Matambalya 1998, Matambalya 1997).

a deeper degree of co-operation with the EU. Besides, to be relevant and ideal development models, EPAs should be able to foster the competitiveness of the respective ACP region or sub-region.

Hence, the consolidation of the regionalisation schemes in the ACP regions and sub-regions should be pursued much more rigorously. The consolidation process should help to fortify intra-country economic reforms and cement regional integration, with the immediate term objective of establishing at least fully functional integration schemes in the ACP regions, prior to embarking on large scale liberalisation against the EU and/or other external partners.

Concretely, to crystallise the prospects of EPAs in fostering viable regional bases for global competitiveness, EPAs should, *inter alia,* (i) foster the utilisation of the economic potentials of the ACP regions and sub-regions by blending the resource potentials and industrialisation objectives, (ii) improve the prospects for the volume and diversification of inward investments (both domestic and foreign), (iii) improve the prospects for the retention of investable surpluses in the region, etc.

10.2. Strategic considerations to enhance competitiveness

In addition to being relevant and ideal as models of development, an EPA should be able to foster the long-term competitiveness of the ACP regions and sub-regions. Hence, strategic considerations are needed with respect to trade and overall economic competitiveness.

10.2.1. Trade competitiveness

A. *Sectoral and product coverage of trade*

To consolidate the prospects of trade benefits, the EPAs should be used to promote global competitiveness in trade. Hence, EPAs should mark a departure from a trade development strategy based on the promotion of the traditional exports (by implication primary products which are less competitive) to the promotion of the non-traditional (in practice) competitive exports that can propel real economic change.

For Eastern and Southern Africa, this means that altogether trade should be used to: (i) foster the utilisation of the region's economic potentials by blending its resource potentials and the diversification of production and trade; (ii) encourage co-operation along competitive rather than protective modalities. The overall objective should be to ease the shift from the current elementary value-adding activities and low value production efforts, to more complex value-adding activities and higher-value production activities in the future.

Also, it is desirable to have a comprehensive trade regime so as to: (i) explicitly address issues related to such "technical barriers to trade" (TBT) as phytosanitary measures, anti-dumping, labour standards and rules of origin, which are likely to be the main trade barriers of the future (ECDPM 1998b); (ii) exploit trade in services, since it constitutes a potential for trade diversification and it is an overall development in many ACP countries. This will be particularly important for small island states which heavily rely on services.

B. Application of asymmetry

Considering the low level of economic development in most ACP economies and the underdeveloped status of the regional integration of their economies, a cautious approach regarding the extent and speed of introducing reciprocity will be needed to attain the goal of EU-ACP integration. The reform programme should be implemented according to clearly defined phases and a realistic timetable. The EU should supportively accompany the ACP integration efforts to full functionality before the introduction of fully functional EU-ACP EPAs. In this context, EPAs should be implemented in two phases:

(a) The first phase should be associated with the extension of more generous preferences to the ACP economies than anticipated under a fully-fledged EPA.

(b) The second phase should involve a fully-fledged FTA between the EU and the relevant ACP regions and sub-regions. It should involve enhancing the free movement of goods, the liberalisation of trade in services, and the free movement of capital.

10.2.2. Overall economic competitiveness

To foster overall economic competitiveness, the EPAs should also address the many supply-side issues, which manifest the real impediments to development. Hence, they should devise the supply-side policies (i.e., policies designed to increase the supply of goods and services to the economies) in order to tackle the supply-side constraints. Concretely, the EPAs should seek to contain constraints related to the human resource base, to the provision of physical infrastructure, to the competitiveness of the private sector, to the empowerment of civil society, and to economic management and governance issues in the broader context.

A. Closing the gap in human resources base

In the long run, in order to create an enabling environment for competitiveness, the ACP economies will need to systematically build *skill-cum-technology* bases. Competitive skill-cum-technology bases will make them attractive for investments and will also attract foreign firms to participate in domestic value adding beyond the elementary levels. In turn, this will help to consolidate the industrialisation programme, regional production cumulation and industrial co-operation

Therefore, the consolidation of the human resources development programme should form an integral part of the economic transformation strategy in the ACP economies. Given its experience and resource base, EU public intervention may be of great help in this area.

B. Closing the gap in the provision of physical infrastructure

Physical infrastructure is a key ingredient in the development process. The need to invest in hardware infrastructure (particularly transport and communications linkages, industrial infrastructure, etc.), as well as in key spheres of software infrastructure, besides the already mentioned human resources development and skill-cum-technology (particularly the development of industrial and commercial services, etc.), is enormously conspicuous in all ACP regions.

It should also be recognised that there exists a link between the stock of human resources and the capacity to maintain physical infrastructure.

C. Improving governance and economic management

Peace and security, together with functioning administrative, legal, and policy frameworks are key prerequisites for the effective utilisation of the opportunities for development. In this regard, they present important facilitators of sustainable development. As hinted not only in the negotiating mandate of the EU, the performance of many ACP economies in these dimensions has been rather discouraging. The call for improvement here is genuine.

Related to good governance are constraints attributable to macro-economic policies. Notably macro-economic policies play a central role as facilitators of investments and trade. Therefore, macro-economic policies should be designed to improve the environment for investment and to support the transformation of the production and export efforts.

D. Empowerment of civil society

In order to rid the EPAs of one of the major flaws of the LC, i.e., a clientele system of linkages between the EU and the ACP elite, it will be necessary to empower civil society. Notably an active civil society acts as a watch dog for societal norms, and therefore has positive influence on economic development. Its empowerment will improve the prospects for its influence on the planning, programming and implementation of development co-operation.

In the ACP countries, civil society can be empowered through promoting a better overall level of literacy and supporting civil society-based organisations. Also, various fora can be established to facilitate the interaction of civil society organisations from the EU and the ACP states.

Though the Commission of the EU in particular underscores the need for greater involvement of non-state actors, so far an official position on how this can be achieved is lacking.

E. Consolidating the private sector

The future EU-ACP co-operation should devote more attention to challenges within the private sector in the ACP regions and design effective support mechanisms to make them competitive in the light of globalisation. Considering the corporate structure in most ACP economies, the programme of co-operation should have special measures to support SMEs. This could be in the form of training aimed at providing management capacities, skills, etc. (ERO 1999).

F. Enhancing capacity to participate in international fora

One of the reasons why the ACP economies have benefited little from the Lomé preferences is their limited capacity to utilise preferences the extended to them, and to participate in other international fora, including the multilateral trade arrangements.[40] In practice, information on Lomé preferences could not easily be diffused to the potential beneficiaries, as the *modus operandi* of the co-operation facilitated the confinement of this information to the hands of a handful government officials (ECDPM 1996, ECDPM 1996b, Matambalya 1999b, Matambalya 1998, Matambalya 1997). To highlight the extent of this problem, according to the final UNIDO report on "Enabling Environment for National Industrial Policy" for Tanzania, the country had resources for one or two officials to cover WTO meetings, while four or five topics were frequently being dealt with in separate meetings at the same time (UNIDO 1999: 22).

Thus, there is a need for capacity building at micro-and macro-levels, to enable the ACP states to identify market opportunities and to utilise them fully. The capacity building should also embrace the regional and sub-regional levels. One area where emphasis should be placed is training for both the public and private sectors. Such training should strategically disseminate knowledge on the various institutions and arrangements relevant for matters of trade and overall economic development, the EU-ACP co-operation, the WTO, the Bretton Woods institutions (i.e., the International Bank for Reconstruction and Development, IBRD, and the International Monetary Fund, i.e., the IMF), such institutions of the United Nations Organisation (UN) as the United Nations Conference on Trade and Development (UNCTAD), the United Nations Industrial Development Organisation (UNIDO), etc.

G. Addressing social equity concerns

Apparently, economic considerations predominate the EPA concept. However, experience shows that liberalisation is associated with a price in terms of shocks that aggravate the hardships of the vulnerable groups of society, like unskilled labour, children and (in many developing countries) women. Therefore, while we, within the framework of regionalised EU-ACP co-operation, pursue reforms aimed at making the ACP economies competitive, we should also think of mechanisms that facilitate socially equitable adjustments, presumably also with EU assistance. This appears to be a necessary condition in order to give credence to EU's role as an "agent of restraint" to "lock-in" reforms and their effects of economic reforms.

In practice, it is hard to see any inward investments forthcoming (and therefore any dynamic gains for the liberalising economy!), in the absence of a critical mass in terms of both quality and quantity of skills-cum-technology. Therefore, in view of the reciprocal opening as per the FTAs, competitiveness based on social equity will also require that we develop the ACP human resource base by training people in skills that will attract investments. Overall, a better-trained workforce will gradually improve income distribution. Also, in the long-run, the approach provides an optional vent for the practical alleviation of mass poverty through carefully planned and enforced liberalisation.

Of course, other rather static forms of compensation could be considered.

---

[40] According to UNIDO (1999: 22), Tanzania, had resources for one or two officials to cover WTO meetings, whereas frequently, four or five topics were being dealt with in separate meetings at the same time.

11. Eastern and Southern Africa and the "geography of regionalisation"

As already pointed out, Eastern and Southern Africa currently hosts a large number of regional integration schemes. Hence, theoretically, it is possible to have separate EPAs with the EAC, the IOC, the SACU, the COMESA, bilateral arrangements with individual states, etc.

However, taking the current situation into consideration and assuming that nothing changes, EPAs will definitely not be implementable with every integration scheme in the region, due to the overlapping membership of countries in these schemes. This obvious barrier can be resolved by making each country decide for membership in only one scheme. The necessity for such a move is also hinted at by the Working Group on Regional Co-operation of the Joint ACP-EU Assembly. Commenting on the status of integration in East Africa, it observes that if progress is to be sustainable, a clearer geographical demarcation between the various regional communities will be required in the medium to long-term (Corrie 1999: 7).

11.1. Alternative options for linking Eastern and Southern Africa and the EU

The criteria for the formation of a viable EPA will greatly depend on the motive for the formation of integration schemes. Considering the evolution of regionalisation efforts in Africa, two considerations are likely to play an influential role on the resultant regional alliances and EPAs, i.e., the *degree of homogeneity of the region* and the *pan-Africanism*.

In conventional terms, the degree of homogeneity stresses such factors as the degree of common interests, shared values, geographical proximity, real economic linkages, etc. among the integrating economies. Thus, it emphasizes the functional merits of integration. Subsequently, the actual country composition of the pertinent integration schemes is driven by economic considerations (Matambalya 1999f). Inherently, the number of members for individual schemes is likely to be small.

The politically flavoured considerations for pan-Africanism stresses integration on a broader base. Since the "geography of regionalisation" targets the rather broader political objectives, the country composition of individual integration schemes is likely to be larger, bringing together countries which are not necessarily closely economically linked (Matambalya 1999f).

11.1.1. "Degree of regional homogeneity" option: EPAs modelled on existing individual integration schemes

Judged on the degree of regional homogeneity, probably only the East African region of Kenya, Tanzania and Uganda, and the Southern African region of South Africa and BLNS may present viable bases for regional alliances on the basis of which EPAs can be formed. The IOC presents another group which, though just beyond its embryonic stage of development, brings together states which have significant commonalties and great potential for a successful integration.

However, it should also clearly be pointed out that even the two most linked subregions Eastern and Southern Africa (i.e., the EAC and SACU respectively), qualify in only some aspects of integration.[41] Overall, they remain far below international standards of what may be recognised as enhanced regional linkages. In addition, they are prone to unbalanced linkages - Kenya dominating in the EAC, while the dominance of South Africa in the SACU is even more conspicuous.

Nevertheless, if judgement is made on strictly economic criteria, it will be plausible for the EU to enter into separate EPA agreements with East Africa (represented by the EAC), Southern Africa (preferably represented by the SADC), and the Small Island States in the Indian Ocean (preferably represented by the IOC).

However, even this approach to geographically grouping the countries of the region will not automatically produce appropriate groupings with which the EU can enter EPA contracts. Notably, member countries of the EAC, IOC, and SADC are prone to overlapping their memberships with memberships of other regionalisation schemes in the region, especially the SACU and COMESA. To complicate matters even further, South Africa has already a separate trade arrangement with the EU.

11.1.2. "Pan-Africanist" option: EPAs modelled on extended regional base

The basic rationale for pan-Africanism in this context would be to build African integration on broader regional bases. The key merits of a pan-Africanist option are:

(a) To overcome the limitations of the market base caused by fragmented African national and even regional markets.

(b) To foster regional solidarity and African unity. In this regard, it conforms with the Abuja Treaty on the formation of the African Economic Community (AEC).

(c) To improve the domestic resource base (and hence provide the critical mass of resources mix) for development in terms of such factors as, markets, capital, etc.

(d) To present relatively strong "integration blocks" in line with contemporary global developments.

There is also another point to support the pan-Africanist approach. This arises from the fact that despite several experiments, integration in Africa is in reality still so underdeveloped that we shall more or less be beginning a new chapter of regional alliances on the continent. Thus, such alliances could be built on a broader base.

Overall, the pan-Africanist approach offers two plausible bases for an EPA, i.e., a broadly based integration scheme for Eastern and Southern Africa (designed to accommodate the countries of the EAC, the IOC, and the SACU) in the form of an "extended" SADC, and a broadly based regionalisation scheme for Eastern and Southern Africa. The two proposals are briefly discussed below.

---

[41] The EAC countries, for instance, are hailed for such factors conducive to effective partnership and regional integration, as common cultures, language and infrastructure (Corrie 1999). However, in terms of such economic dimensions as capital flows, intra-regional movement of people, regional infrastructure and institutional linkages, the SACU economies are comparatively more advanced.

A. *"Pan-Africanist" option 1: co-operation under the "extended" SADC umbrella*

The first possible scenario involving a "pan-Africanist" option is an EPA between the EU and a broadly based integration scheme, but confined to Eastern and Southern Africa as defined in this study. In this regard, an "extended" SADC, accommodating within it all the countries of the EAC, the IOC and the SACU, together with the remaining SADC members which do not belong to any of these groups, could be considered. In such an arrangement, the EAC, the IOC, and the SACU would form the three growth poles of the region (i.e., the "extended" SADC).

This option will have several additional advantages. Besides having political appeal, technically it also offers mechanisms to address the complexity associated with the rather amorphous alliances in the region. To take care of the various economic interests, the strategy of variable geometry which allows some members to integrate faster than others, could then be applied in the relations among the three sub-groups of the "extended" SADC, i.e., the EAC, the IOC and the SACU.

Also, by adopting this approach, South Africa may be accommodated in the group. In this context, following the logic that if LLDCs can benefit from SDT within or outside an EPA, it should also be possible to treat a more advanced state like South Africa differently. For instance, variable geometry regarding RSA-EU linkages on the one hand, and the EU and the remaining countries of the group on the other hand, may be practised.

Besides, a regionalisation scheme based on an "extended" SADC as envisaged in this case, will consolidate regional solidarity, while at the same time accommodating the diversifying interests of the countries of the region (which can continue to work together through the EAC, the IOC, and the SACU).

B. *"Pan-Africanist" option 2: co-operation under "extended" context of Eastern and Southern Africa*

The macro-and micro- economic characteristics of Africa suggest that regionalisation on an even broader basis may provide the answer to some of the more challenging questions with regard to economic development. In this context, extending the concept further, it may be possible to integrate within this group not only the states from the Horn of Africa (i.e., Ethiopia, Eritrea, Djibouti, and Somalia), but also Burundi and Rwanda, without them having to belong to any integration scheme (in this case, the EAC, the IOC and the SACU).

In this case as well, there will be advantages in terms of market considerations, of domestic resource bases, and of overall long-term political appeal. Additionally, analogous to the approach under "extended" SADC, variable geometry may be used to consolidate solidarity within the existing regionalisation schemes.

11.2. Summarising remarks

It is obvious that making the decisions on the "geography of regionalisation" in Africa will be a rather tough task, requiring ingenuity and a lot of strategic thinking and compromising. Informed opinion on the merits and demerits of each approach will be a necessary input to the decision-making exercise. In this regard, it will be necessary not to pre-judge any of the models, but to constructively and seriously consider the merits and demerits of each, as well as their practicability in the current setting in the concerned regions and the international system as a whole.

The comparison of an EPA based on "degree of regional homogeneity" and one based on "pan-Africanist" considerations would appear to bring out a number of factors that weigh in favour of the latter model. The shortcomings of the African economies necessitate co-operation on a broader regional basis. In this context, the possibility of dividing Africa South of the Sahara into two major regions (Eastern and Southern Africa, and Central and Western Africa) for the purpose of EPAs, while retaining the existing regionalisation schemes in these broad regions, should be explored. These broadly defined regions (i.e., Eastern and Southern Africa, and Central and Western Africa) can also be linked through a set of arrangements.

12. Concluding remarks

The *Framework Agreement* provides the broad guidelines on which future EU-ACP co-operation will be based. However, the actual form of the co-operation is still nebulous with respect to many aspects. Hence, as we prepare ourselves for the negotiations about the details of the co-operation, there is an urgent need to seriously deliberate on concrete details of the envisaged EPAs.

In this study, we set out to explore the prospects for future EU-ACP links, with focus on Eastern and Southern Africa. In the analysis, we illuminated the subject in relation to other important aspects of the negotiations. We come to the conclusion that an EPA does in fact provide an innovative model of development co-operation, more appropriate for the creation and enhancement of sustainable ACP competitiveness. On the whole, the advantages of this model are underlined by several benefits of both a static nature (e.g., static *welfare gains* in terms of price advantages) and a dynamic nature (e.g., the creation of a conducive environment in which to *foster positive shifts in investment and production*, systematic *upward convergence* resulting from the merging of the ACP economies with the high performance EU economies, and *increased global competitiveness* in the long-run due to competitive restructuring). In addition, an EPA will improve prospects for *"locking-in" reforms* in the ACP economies.

However, particularly in the short-run, an EPA will be burdened by *fiscal losses* (e.g., loss of government revenues due to foregone customs revenues and an eroded revenue base) and *negative dynamic effects* (e.g., negative shifts in domestic investments and production like the crowding out of domestic investments, the enhancement of one-sided dependence due to the diversion of investments from third countries, etc.). In addition there will be *adjustment costs of liberalisation* (e.g., economic restructuring, general reduction of economic activity, unemployment, development of alternative sources of revenues, etc.).

The fact that the ACP economies are less developed than the EU economies suggests further that, in the short-run, the costs (for the ACP economies) will surpass the benefits. To alleviate the burden for the ACP economies, there is a need for intervention in terms of supportive policies and compensation mechanisms. The former will depend on the creation of necessary conditions for positive dynamic effects which will in the long-run lead to *upward convergence* in the ACP regions and sub-regions. The latter will continue to rely on static transfers from the EU into the ACP states.

In general, the ACP economies need to clearly study the meaning and impact of EPAs, to consider the merits of the EPA model, and to proceed to actively influencing its configuration. Though there is no co-operation arrangement that is one hundred percent comparable to the proposed EPAs, some existing arrangements offer insight as to what to expect. A study of the EU's Mediterranean regime and, more relevant, the NAFTA, may offer answers to many questions and provide the necessary information input for the better planning of EPAs.

Considering the available options, EPAs based on a *multi-level, multi-tier co-operation arrangement* present the most appealing course of action. This will contain both a *global level* component, and *regional level* component. The global level component will retain the global platform for co-operation between the EU and its ACP associates as a group. It could also possibly include within the ACP group, other nations at the same level of development from the respective regions. It will specify the general undertakings and focus on the issues identified for the agenda for development co-operation.

The *regional level* components will constitute a series of bilateral agreements between the EU and the respective ACP regions and sub-regions (e.g., Eastern and Southern Africa, Central and Western Africa, Caribbean, Pacific), or existing integration schemes (e.g., EAC, IOC, SACU, SADC). It will focus on the regional co-operation agenda.

The resultant *two-level, multi-tier* EU-ACP links will ensure the preservation of the historic EU-ACP links, while at the same time enhancing the economic efficiency of the links in future. In this context, it will boost the overall efficiency of the development co-operation.

Inasmuch as EPAs necessitate integration in the ACP regions, they should make use of the experience of integration schemes which already exist. With particular reference to Eastern and Southern Africa, we suggest serious consideration of three options:

(a) Separate EPAs with the EAC, IOC, and SADC.

(b) An EPA on the basis of an "extended" SADC to accommodate the EAC, IOC and SACU. Within this framework, variable geometry can be practised to enable the already co-operating economies to pursue closer integration under the EAC, IOC, and SACU.

(c) An EPA on the basis of an extended co-operation in Eastern and Southern Africa to accommodate also the states of the Horn of Africa, as well as Burundi and Rwanda. Within this broader co-operation framework, variable geometry can also be practised.

The ACP economies together with their EU associates should critically consider the viable "geography of regionalisation", particularly in Africa. Whether or not any regionalisation scheme will work will depend on the reality on the ground and the political will.

Regardless of the form that they will eventually take, the success of EPAs will depend on the extent to which the key actors will recognise that it is essential to focus development co-operation efforts on eliminating or minimising the supply side deficits, which remain strong in the overwhelming majority of the ACP economies. Among other things, it must be noted that:

(i) Preferences are just one of many explanatory variables in the *development equation*, and probably not the most important ones in the contemporary context.

(ii) Past experience suggests that any development co-operation model that does not take into account the diversity of development deterrents will not be able to deliver the desired results. Apparently (and probably more important), the diverse supply side constraints (e.g., deficits in physical infrastructure, human resources, information and communication infrastructure, deficient national social capital, deficits in the national building process, fractionalisation of state institutions as well as of institutions in the civil society, etc.), more adequately portray the sources for the underdevelopment of the ACP economies.

(iii) Capacity building focusing on strengthening regionalisation schemes as well as public and private institutions will have the best chance, as a long-term solution. This is because they depend on the situation on the ground (e.g., state of national social capital, technological and educational base of the country, etc.). Therefore focusing too much effort on capacity building in the short term may lead to a fate similar to that of a solid roof constructed on top of a weak foundation.

It remains to be seen whether the Eastern and Southern African and other ACP economies can capitalise on the provisions of a masterpiece of *Framework Agreement*, and negotiate and effectively implement mutually beneficial EPAs.

V APPENDIXES

Appendix I : Proposed multi-tier regionally differentiated EU-ACP linkages

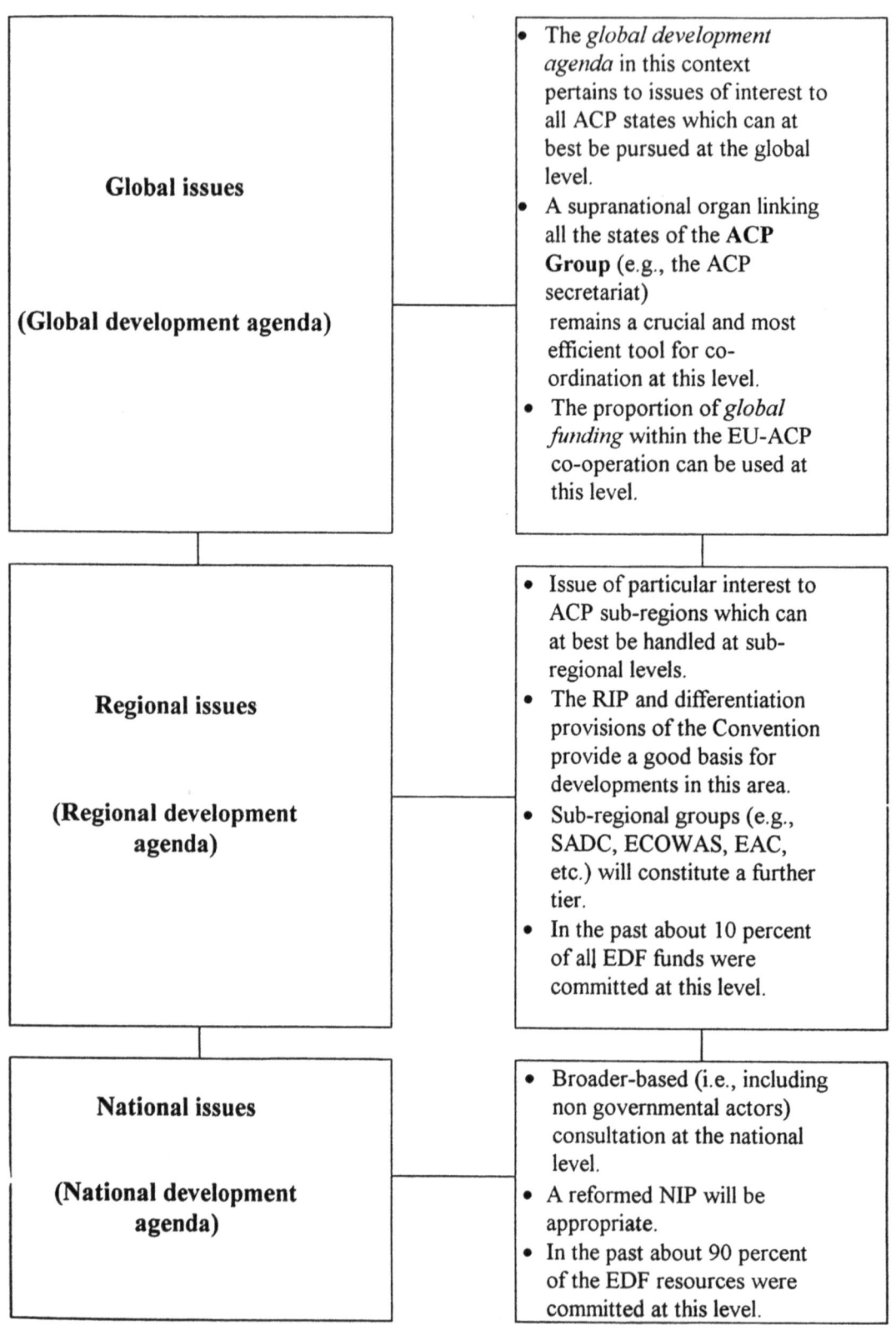

Appendix II : Key staff requirements of a reformed ACP secretariat

Position	Officers reporting to her/him
Secretary General	• Deputy Secretary General • Directors of the following GDs 　　* *GD I*: Trade and Economic Co-operation 　　* *GD II*: Investments and Private Sector Development 　　* *GD III*: Financial Co-operation 　　* *GD IV*: Political Co-operation 　　* *GD V*: Information and Statistics
Deputy Secretary General	• Directors of the following (hypothetical) RDs 　　* *RD A*: CARIBBEAN 　　* *RD B*: EAC 　　* *RD C*: ECOWAS 　　* *RD D*: HORN 　　* *RD E*: SADC 　　* *RD F*: UEMOA 　　* *RD G*: PACIFIC or 　　* *RD A*: CARIBBEAN 　　* *RD B*: EASTERN AND SOUTHERN AFRICA (i.e., SADC II) 　　* *RD C*: CENTRAL AND WEST AFRICA 　　* *RD D*: PACIFIC or According to any other preferred "geography of regionalisation"•
Directors of GDs	• Experts and supporting staff
Directors of RDs	• Country Desk Officers • Experts and supporting staff
Country Desk Officers	• According to organisational structure

Notes:
GD ... General Directorate
RD ... Regional Directorate
CEMAC ... Communauté Économique et Monétaire de l'Afrique Centrale.
ECOWAS ... Economic Community for West African States.
CARIBBEAN ... Caribbean ACP states (e.g., extended CARICOM to include Haiti and Cuba).
Horn ... Horn of Africa (presumably, Djibouti, Ethiopia, Eritrea, Somalia).
SADC ... Southern African Development Community.
SADC II ... Extended SADC including EAC, IOC, SACU.
UEMOA ... Union Économique et Monétaire Ouest-Africaine.
PACIFIC ... Pacific ACP states. i.e., Fiji, Kiribati, Tonga, Papua New Guinea, Samoa, Solomon Islands, Tuvalu, and Vanuatu.

Appendix III: The Cotonou Agreement and what it means for Tanzania

For the wide spectrum of stakeholders in every individual member of the ACP group, it is important to grasp the implications of the New Cooperation Between Agreement between the EU and ACP-States, enshrined in the Cotonou Agreement.

Some of the pressing questions of great relevance for Tanzanians of all walks of life are: What is it that really comes after the Lomé Convention? Why was a new Agreement needed? What are the "pillars" and the major innovations of the new Agreement? What does it mean for Tanzania?

In this appendix, we briefly highlight some answers to these questions

A. What is it the Cotonou Agreement about?

On 3 February 3 2000, the eighteen months of negotiations between the EU and the ACP group of nations were concluded and enshrined in the *Framework Agreement*. This agreement, which was ceremoniously signed in Cotonou, the capital of Gabon, on 23 June 2000 is also referred to as the *Cotonou Agreement*.

The new ACP-EU partnership agreement is for a twenty-year period (2000-2020). It contains a significantly reformed aid package to support development and poverty reduction. Without trying to dissolve the ACP group of nations, the Agreement also provides a basis for the formulation between the EU and ACP states (individually or as groups) of what is referred to as the *Economic Partnerships Agreements* (EPAs). Within this new context of EU-ACP development co-operation, the ACP and EU will jointly seek to, among other things, to harness regional growth, promote new trade regimes (i.e., trade agreements) which should be compatible with the stipulations of the World Trade Organisation (WTO). They also declare their intentions to foster political commitment to promote good governance and stability in the ACP countries.

The financial protocol of the new partnership agreement will be revised every five years. The protocol sets the amount of the European Development Fund (EDF) - which is financed by EU member states and administered by the European Commission (EC). During 2000-2005 the EDF 9 amounts to EURO 13.5 billion (equivalent to Tanzanian Shillings 88 billion). Besides, there will be EURO 1.7 billion from European Investment Bank (EIB) resources. Also, the EURO 9.5 billion not spent from previous EDFs will be added to this amount. In sum, these present the resources which will be available for distribution among the 77 ACP states associated with the EU through the Cotonou Agreement.

The Cotonou Agreement builds on some experiences of the Lomé Conventions, with their respect for social, economic, political and human rights and aid and trade concessions. However, the way financial support is given has been simplified and there will be a new focus on trade to meet the new millennium's challenges - globalisation, liberalisation, regional integration and the promotion of a market economy. This will make the agreement better equipped to stimulate economic growth and reduce poverty.

B. Why was a new agreement needed?

The end of the Lomé IV Agreement in February 2000 was the opportunity for deeper changes to EU-ACP co-operation, partly addressing its merits and demerits, and partly adjusting to the significantly changed realities in the international system of relations. The backdrop was that, in view of the experiences with the Lomé Convention, the ACP-EU co-operation could do better and needed to adapt to a different geo-strategic situation after the demise of the East-West ideological blocks. Among other things, the Cotonou Agreement explicitly underscores the resolve by the EU and ACP states to:

o Enhance the political dimension of co-operation.
o Address corruption, blamed for blocking the achievement of development goals in many ACP states.
o Promote participatory approaches in designing and implementing development co-operation. In this line, the stronger involvement of civil society in the reforms and policies to be supported by EU is underlined.
o Refocus development policies on poverty reduction strategies.
o Base the allocation of funds not only on an assessment of each country's needs but also of its policy performance.
o Create an investment facility to support the development of the private sector.
o Rationalise instruments and introduce a new system of rolling programming, allowing the Community and the beneficiary country to regularly adjust their co-operation programme
o Decentralise administrative, and in some cases financial, responsibilities to local level with the aim of making co-operation more effective.
o Improve the policy framework for trade and investment development.
o Enhance co-operation in all areas important to trade, including new issues such as labour standards and the linkages between environment and trade.

C. What are the pillars of the Cotonou Agreement?

The new Agreement clearly defines a perspective that combines politics, trade and development. In an extended sense, the Cotonou Agreement is based on five interdependent pillars:

o Comprehensive political dimension
o Participatory approaches
o Strengthened focus on poverty reduction
o New framework for economic and trade co-operation
o Reform of financial co-operation

Reflecting the international debate on poverty reduction, the partnership seeks to provide an enabling framework for ACP development strategies, ensuring complementarity and interaction between the economic, social, cultural, gender, institutional and environmental dimensions of policies and strategies.

D. What will it mean for Tanzania?

Like other ACP Countries, there is potential for Tanzania to benefit from a carefully formulated and implemented EPA, particularly in the long run. Notably, it will take time before those effects are visible. The new Head of the EU Delegation in Dar es Salaam, William Hanna, sees the Cotonou Agreement as a major step forward in improving the way that the EU provides assistance to Tanzania. He describes it as a complete overhaul of procedures and financial instruments to accelerate disbursements of development aid.

The other big change for Tanzania will be that all the aid will come together out of one fund.

Already members of the Tanzanian government and civil society representatives have been invited to meetings to help them become better informed about Cotonou. The EU/Tanzania Country Support Strategy should be ready in the first months of 2001, and a new agreement between Tanzania and the EC should be signed by the middle of the year. (EU Delegation Tanzania 2001).

You can find the Cotonou Agreement in English and the compendium of guidelines proposed for its implementation by the Commission:
http://europa.eu.int/comm/development/cotonou/index_en.htm
http://europa.eu.int/eur-lex/en/com/pdf/2000/com2000_0424en01.pdf

E. Some critical views

The reception of the Cotonou Agreement has been received with mixed feelings. Among the institutions which find it faulty are the World Economy, Ecology and Development (WEED) and Terre des Hommes. Detailed information on their position can be read on weed@weedbonn.org and terre@t-online.de

They note that: "Our reaction to the outcome of the negotiations between the EU and the ACP states was conflicting. A comprehensive reform of the Lomé Convention has not taken place. The former agreement's strength, which consisted of a tight connection between development aid and trade cooperation, has finally succumbed to the rules of free world trade".

They further argue that "the focus of the future EU-ACP-relations will be the so-called economy partnership settlements, which are to be agreed upon by the EU and groups of ACP countries within the next 8 years. The EU's main objective is to improve access to the market in developing countries for European companies."

Selected references

ACP: "EU-ACP Negotiation Information Memo No 10: Conclusions of the Brussels ministerial conference held on 2 and 3 February 2000", Brussels, 2000.

ACP: "Press Release of the ACP Group in the Aftermath of the Conclusion of the Framework Agreement to Guide EU-ACP Co-operation", February 2000.

ACP (1998): "WTO compatibility and the future of ACP-EU Agreements", Brussels, 1998.

ACP/EU: "Partnership Agreement between the African, Caribbean and Pacific States and the European Union and its member States", February 2000.

ACP: "ACP Group Negotiating Mandate", ACP /28/028/98Rev. 2 Neg., Brussels, 1998.

ACP: "The Libreville Declaration", ACP /28/05/97(Final), Brussels, 1997.

AG Development Co-operation of the SPD: "EU Enlargement and Development Co-operation", Brussels, 1999.

Bheenick, R.: "Investment Protection and Promotion in the ACP-EU Context", ECDPM Working Paper No. 43, Maastricht, 1997.

Box, L. and von Braun, J.: "Looking Beyond Lomé IV: Towards Practice-Oriented Policies", ZEF, GEMDEV, ECDPM, 1999.

Buitelaar, R.: "Dynamic Gains from Intra-regional Trade in Latin America" in Belous, R. and Lemco, J. (Eds)"NAFTA as a Model of Development: The Benefits and Costs of Merging High and Low Wage Areas", National Planning Associates / Friedrich-Ebert-Foundation / Institute of the Americas, 1993.

Cohen, I.: "The NAFTA and the Downward Wage Pressure" in Belous, R. and Lemco, J. (Eds) "NAFTA as a Model of Development: The Benefits and Costs of Merging High and Low Wage Areas", National Planning Associates / Friedrich-Ebert-Foundation / Institute of the Americas, 1993.

Collier, P., Guillaumont, P., Guillaumont, S., Gunning, J.: "The Future of Lomé: Europe's Role in African Growth", CSAE (Oxford University), CERDI (University of Auvergne), Free University of Amsterdam, 1997.

Corrie, J.: "Draft Report on Regional Co-operation in the ACP Countries", Report by the Rapporteur of the Working Group on Regional Co-operation in the ACP Countries, of the ACP-EU Joint Assembly, 1999.

CREDIT: "Study on the Economic Impact of Introducing Reciprocity into the Trade Relations between the EU and EAC Countries", Final Report Prepared for the

EU, 1998.

ECDPM: "Debating Future Co-operation Between Europe, Africa, the Caribbean, and the Pacific", Lomé 2000, ECDPM, Maastricht, 1999a.

ECDPM: "Lomé 2000: Debating future co-operation between Europe, Africa, the Caribbean and the Pacific", No. 12, November 1999.

ECDPM: "Towards an ACP Position: Exploring ACP Responses to the EU Proposal for Regional Economic Partnership Agreements", Lomé Negotiating Brief No. 4, ECDPM, Maastricht, 1998a.

ECDPM: "What Future for ACP-EU Trade Relations?", Lomé Negotiating Brief No. 1, ECDPM, Maastricht, 1998b.

ECDPM: "Synthesis of Working Group Discussions on the Future of EU-ACP Relations Beyond the Lomé IV Convention", Maastricht, 1996a.

ECDPM: "Position Papers on the Future of EU-ACP Relations Beyond the Lomé IV Convention", Maastricht, 1996b.

ECDPM: "What Future for ACP-EU Trade Relations?", Lomé Negotiating Brief, ECDPM, Maastricht, 1998.

ERO: "What does the recent ACP-EU agreement mean for Southern Africa's future trade relations with the EU?", ERO 2000.

EU Delegation in Tanzania: "European Union News, Tanzania", January 2001.

European Commission: "Green Paper on Relations between the European Union and the Countries on the Eve of the 21st century: Challenges and Options for a New Partnership", European Commission, Directorate General VIII, Brussels, 1996.

European Commission (1999): "Next Stage: Ministerial Conference in Dakar, 8 and 9", EU-ACP.

EU Negotiating Group (1999): "ACP-EU Negotiations: Group 3 - Trade and Commercial Co-operation Speaking Notes", CE/TFN/GCEC3/09-EN, Brussels.

EU Negotiating Group (1999): "An Analysis of Trends in Lomé IV Trade Regime and the Consequences for Retaining It", CE/TFN/GCEC3/09-EN, Brussels.

EU: "Green Paper on Relations between the European Union and the ACP Countries on the Eve of the 21st Century: Challenges and Options for a New Partnership" EU-ACP European Commission, Directorate General VIII, Brussels, 1996.

Goodison, P.: "National Perspectives on Post-Lomé IV Debate: A Swaziland Case Study", ECDPM Working Paper No. 62, Maastricht, 1998.

Graumans, A. (1999): "Political Dialogue Between the EU and the SADC: Insights for ACP-EU Dialogue", ECDPM Working Paper No. 61, Maastricht.

Grynberg, R.: "Negotiating a Fait Accompli: The WTO Incompatibility of Lomé Convention Trade Provisions and the ACP-EU Negotiations", ECDPM Working Papers No. 38, ECDPM, Maastricht, 1997.

IDIL: "Study on the Impact of Introducing Reciprocity into the Trade Relations between the EU and the SADC region", Final Report Prepared for the EU, 1998.

IDS: "Study on the Impact of Introducing Reciprocity into the Trade Relations between the EU and CARICOM/Dominican Republic", Final Report Prepared for the EU, 1998.

IOC: "The Future of the Indian Ocean Commission: Strategic Reflections on Regional Co-operation in the Next Ten Years", White Paper, IOC, ECDPM, EU, 1998.

Koulaimah-Gabriel, A.: "Beyond Lomé IV: Future Challenges of EU-Africa Relations", ECDPM Working Paper No. 7, Maastricht, 1997.

Langhammer R., Hiemenz, U.:"Regional Integration Among Developing Countries: Opportunities, Obstacles, Options", J.C.B. Mohr (Paul Siebeck), Tübingen, 1990.

Lingnau, H.: "Perspectives on Lomé Convention", ECDPM Working Paper No. 12, ECDPM, Maastricht.

Gonzales, A. "The Caribbean-EU Relations in a Post-Lomé World", Friedrich-Ebert-Stiftung, Bonn, 1996.

Gonzales, P., Antonio, G., Lafontaine, O., Peres, S., Schröder, G., et al: "Shaping Globalisation", Friedrich-Ebert-Foundation, Bonn, 1999.

Kit, D.: "Regional integration and development in Southern Africa: The implications of the reciprocal free trade agreement with the EU", Koordination Suedliches Afrika, Bonn, 1999.

Matambalya, F.: "The Merits and Demerits of EU Policies Towards Associated Developing Countries", 2nd revised edition, Peter Lang Publishers, Frankfurt an Main . Berlin . Bern . New York . Paris . Vienna, 1999a.

Matambalya, F.: "Post-Lomé IV EU-ACP Relations and Prospects for Regionalised and Multi-tier EU-ACP Co-operation Arrangements", Political Dialogue Paper of the Consultative Group on Lomé Convention (CGLC) and Friedrich-Ebert-Stiftung, Dar es Salaam, 1999b.

Matambalya, F.: "Making the GSP the Second Best Option", paper presented at the SADC Workshop on Negotiations on Post-Lomé IV, co-organised by the SADC Secretariat and Friedrich-Ebert-Foundation, Harare, 10 - 11 May 1999c.

Matambalya, F.: "Post-Lomé IV ACP EU Relations and the Prospects for Regionalised and Multi-tier EU-ACP Co-operation"" Unpublished field survey, Brussels/Dar es Salaam, 1999d.

Matambalya, F.: "Private Investments - A Crucial Factor for Growth and Competitiveness?" in Wolf, S. (Ed.) "The Future of EU-ACP Relations", Peter Lang Science Publishers, Bern . Berlin . Frankfurt . New York . Paris . Vienna, 1999e.

Matambalya, F.: "Economic Policies and Economic Reform Process in Tanzania: Critical Evaluation of Past Experiences in Integration Schemes and Perspectives for the Future", paper presented at the Symposium "Tanzania Revisited: Political Stability, Aid Dependency and Development Constraints", Hamburg, 22-23 October, 1999f.

Matambalya, F.: "Future Perspectives of EU-ACP Relations: The Case of Southern African States", Friedrich-Ebert-Foundation, Bonn, 1998.

Matambalya, F.: "The Impact of Regionalisation Schemes on the Export and Economic Performance of Developing Countries: A Case Study of the Southern African Development Community (SADC)", Brandes and Apsel/Südwind, Frankfurt a. Main/ Vienna, 1995.

Matambalya, F. and Wolf, S.: "The Cotonou Agreement and the Challenges of making it WTO Compatible" (forthcoming), Journal of World Trade, Vol. Number 34, February.

McQueen, M.: "The impact studies on the effects of REPAs between the ACP and the EU", ECDPM Discussion Paper No. 3, Maastricht, 1999.

McQueen, M.: "ACP-EU Trade Co-operation After the Year 2000: An assessment of reciprocal trade preferences", Journal of Modern African Studies, 3, 4, 1998: 669-692.

Minford, P.: "Markets Not Stakes: The Triumph of Capitalism and Stakeholder Fallacy", Orion Business Books, London, 1998.

NEI: "Introducing Reciprocity into the Trade Relations between the EU and Pacific ACP Countries", Final Report Prepared for the EU, 1998.

Page, S., Robinson, P, Solignac-Lecomte, H.B. and Bussolo, M.: "SADC-EU Trade Relations in a Post- Lomé World", Overseas Development Institute, 1999.

Reynolds, C.: "The NAFTA and the Wage Convergence: A Case of Winners and Losers" in Belous, R. and Lemco, J.: (Eds): "NAFTA as a Model of Development?", National Planning Association, Institute of the America, Friedrich-Ebert-Stiftung, 1993.

Solignac-Lecomte, H-B.: "Options for Future ACP-EU Trade Relations", European Centre for Development Policy Management, ECDPM Working Paper No. 60, Maastricht 1998.

Thomas, R.: "The WTO and Trade Co-operation between the ACP and the EU: Assessing the Options?", ECDPM, 1997.

WEED/Terre des Hommes: "Co-operation between the EU and the ACP States: The Cotonou Agreement", www.weedbonn.org, terre@t-online.de, 2000.

Whiting Jr.,van R.: "Dynamic Integration, Foreign Investments and Open Regionalism in the NAFTA and the Americas" in Belous, R. and Lemco, J.: (Eds): "NAFTA as a Model of Development?", National Planning Association, Institute of the America, Friedrich-Ebert-Stiftung, 1993.

About the Author and Series Editor

Dr. Francis A.S.T. Matambalya is a Senior Lecturer in the Faculty of Commerce and Management of the University of Dar es Salaam, Tanzania where he has served in various capacities, amongst others as Associate Dean for Research and Publications. Currently, he is a Humboldt Scholar and Senior Fellow at the Center for Development Research (ZEF) of Bonn University (Germany). He is also the Interim Co-ordinator of the CGDC.

Dr. Matambalya has a Bachelor of Commerce Degree (Marketing Major) from the University of Dar es Salaam, an M.Sc. in Business Administration (with a major in Marketing and Business Informatics) from the Johannes Kepler University Linz (Austria), and a Ph.D. (International Economic Relations) from the Ruhr-University Bochum (Germany). He has authored two books, co-authored two books, and has published several articles in the field of international economic relations in general and trade economics in particular.

Policy Dialogue Papers of the Friedrich-Ebert-Stiftung, Tanzania

1. *Francis A.S.T. Matambalya*
Post-Lomé IV EU-ACP Relations and Prospects for Regionalised and Multi-tier EU-ACP Co-operation Arrangements

2. *Stefan Mair*
The German African Policy with Focus on East Africa (Unpublished paper)

3. *Erold Arduc*
The German Basic Law (Unpublished paper)

Friedrich Ebert Stiftung ("Stiftung" being the German for "foundation"), was founded as a political legacy of Germany's first democratically elected president, Friedrich Ebert, who died in that year. Ebert was a Social Democrat of humble origins who had risen to the highest office in his country despite considerable opposition from his political adversaries. He assumed the burden of the presidency in a country which was crisis ridden, following its defeat in World War I. His own personal experience led him to propose the establishment of a foundation with a threefold aim:

- to further a democratic, pluralistic, political culture by means of political education for all classes of society.
- to facilitate the access of gifted young people to higher education by providing scholarships.
- to contribute to international understanding and cooperation wherever possible in order to avert a fresh outbreak of war and conflict.

To-day the Friedrich Ebert Stiftung is a political, non-profit making, public interest institution committed to the principles and basic values of social democracy in its educational and policy-oriented work.

Development cooperation

In the FES offices in Africa, Asia, Latin America and Oceania approximately 100 German staff and 600 local nationals are involved in projects in the fields of economic and social development, social-political education and information, the media and communication and in providing advisory services.

FES sees its activities in the developing countries as a contribution to:
- the improvement of political and social framework conditions
- the democratisation of the social structure
- the empowerment of women and the promotion of gender awareness
- the strengthening of free trade unions
- the improvement of communication and media structures
- regional and international media cooperation
- regional cooperation between states and interest groups
- the resolution of the North-South conflict

Friedrich Ebert Stiftung
Kawawa Road, Plot 397
P.O.Box 4472
Dar es Salaam, Tanzania

Tel: 00255 - 22 2668575 / 2668786
Fax: 00255 - 22 2668669
Mobile: 0742 785 434 / 0741 324 924
E-mail: fes@fes-tz.org
Internet: www.fes-tz.org

www.ingramcontent.com/pod-product-compliance
Lightning Source LLC
Chambersburg PA
CBHW080254030426
42334CB00023BA/2817